THE COHERENCE

OF

Wisdom

A Parascriptural Gospel Narrative

DR. CHUCK CADLE

WESTBOW
PRESS®
A DIVISION OF THOMAS NELSON
& ZONDERVAN

WestBow Press books may be ordered through booksellers or by contacting:

WestBow Press
A Division of Thomas Nelson & Zondervan
1663 Liberty Drive
Bloomington, IN 47403
www.westbowpress.com
844-714-3454

Scripture quotations taken from The Holy Bible, New International Version® NIV® Copyright © 1973 1978 1984 2011 by Biblica, Inc. TM. Used by permission. All rights reserved worldwide.

ISBN: 978-1-6642-1039-4 (sc)
ISBN: 978-1-6642-1041-7 (hc)
ISBN: 978-1-6642-1040-0 (e)

Library of Congress Control Number: 2020921111

Print information available on the last page.

WestBow Press rev. date: 05/25/2021

CONTENTS

DEDICATIONS

I want to thank Elaine, my beloved wife, for her enduring love and support.

I will always cherish my children, Alicia, Jeff, and Jason, who gave me so many precious memories and for blessing Elaine and me with grandchildren.

I will remember my parents and grandparents for their love and nurture.

Lastly, I would like to acknowledge my Heavenly Father, who has provided me with the freedom to take chances and make choices, and who gave me the strength and faith to persevere through hardships.

ACKNOWLEDGMENTS

I wish to thank Mr. Eric Wolff for his consultation and advice in writing this manuscript. Mr. Wolff served as my executive mentor for eight years. His mentorship, guidance, consultation, and friendship have meant the world to me. Mr. Wolff is a successful entrepreneur who understands the importance of perseverance, grit, and mission-driven actions.

I wish to thank Dr. Nancy Wingenbach for her inspiration to pursue my Doctorate in Education, as it was her encouragement that enabled me to achieve my goal. She retired as a school superintendent of Orange County Schools in Ohio and served as a Board Trustee for Destination Imagination, Inc. (DI) during my tenure with the company. Her academic knowledge and experience, along with her passion for student learning, provided me a valuable perspective in leading DI.

I wish to thank Mr. Mark Rein for helping me build value in UtiliCom Networks and being a special friend and advocate. Mr. Rein is now the CIO for the U.S. International Development Finance Corporation in Washington, DC.

Finally, I wish to think Ms. Elaine Cadle, my awesome wife, for her assistance in writing this manuscript. Her many constructive comments, edits, and suggestions were valued and appreciated. This book would not have been possible without her support.

INTRODUCTION

Get wisdom, get understanding; do not forget my words
or turn away from them. Do not forsake wisdom, and she
will protect you; love her, and she will watch over you.
—Proverbs 4:5–6

Have you ever wondered what compels someone to write? I get curious every time I see a new monograph in my areas of interest. What might I learn from it, and does the author have a perspective different from my own? Sometimes, I will download a book excerpt from Amazon to discern the impetus that propelled the author to commit countless days to write. My explorations are also a way to meet these accomplished writers through their work. I seek to learn about their personality, their interests, who inspired them, their education and experience, and how might I benefit from their written work or dismiss it as inferior or unavailing information. From these explorations, I hope to gain new knowledge and wisdom.

Today we have access to so many scholarly and light reading books, magazines, scholarly articles, newsletters, and Internet blogs. Each of these works enables us to expand our vocabulary, research a topic, challenge our assumptions, and increase our subject-matter understanding. First, however, we should ask ourselves, "how do we ascertain what is truth instead of conjecture or misleading information?"

In school and most educational venues, we customarily have

a teacher in the front of the room guiding our academic growth by teaching us "what to think," but not "how to think." I believe hermeneutics should be a required course in school to ensure students have the opportunity to practice and learn discernment principles.

Writing this manuscript has taken me the better part of a year. If you are reading this introduction, you should know that you are reading a reprint of the earlier published version. After the initial release, I noticed several errors, corrected them, and then had the book republished. In thinking of the time spent on this manuscript, I assume, like me, writers persevere because they believe the world will be a better place because we told our story.

You will notice that at the start of each chapter, I have included a Bible verse to set the stage for my upcoming dialogue, and this verse and all verses within this manuscript are from the New International Version (NIV) Bible. If you like these verses and would like to know more about my Christian beliefs, please visit this book's website for a bonus chapter: www.thecoherenceofwisdom.com. If you have a chance, I would love to hear from you about your journey and life discoveries, so please leave comments and book reviews on the website.

I have had many unique, fascinating, rewarding, and challenging opportunities in my life. Hopefully, my reflective effort to share my life lessons will provide a perspective that may benefit you in some meaningful way. This book's title, The Coherence of Wisdom, came to me as I evaluated my life journey. Looking back, it is now easy to see why I ventured down different paths. The choices I made and the chances I took each produced an outcome. When evaluated together as a unified whole, these individual outcomes have provided me with the coherence of wisdom. Lessons learned from early childhood trauma through today have enabled me to gain insight from my different interactions with life events. This wisdom includes self-knowledge of my strengths and weaknesses. Self-knowledge is a crucial attribute of wisdom.

In this autobiography, I will be sharing my life stories with you with three goals in mind: that you may gain wisdom from my lessons learned; that you understand the importance of self-awareness, self-knowledge, self-efficacy, and resilience; and that you see the importance of having God and His words to guide you in life choices. In addition, people can gain wisdom and insight from understanding the decision-making processes of others. I trust that this book will become a helpful resource as you discern the coherence of wisdom from your life events.

Let's have a conversation.

CHAPTER 1

A Firm Foundation

Start children off on the way they should go, and even
when they are old, they will not turn from it.

—PROVERBS 22:6

hroughout my life, I have encountered the term "wisdom." The book of Proverbs puts such a significant emphasis on gaining it that I feel it is necessary to define this word before going any further. In chapter 9 of the book, *A Handbook of Wisdom* (Sternberg & Jordan, 2011, p. 16), Robert Sternberg defines wisdom as follows: "Wisdom is a metacognitive style plus sagacity {good judgment}, knowing that one does not know everything, seeking the truth to the extent that it is knowable." I like this definition, as it reminds me that choices are individual decisions. We can learn from exploring these choices as they allow us to examine our interactions with others and gain situational knowledge and experience from these interactions. This investigated knowledge and experience leads to coherence. Wisdom comes from knowing when and how to use this coherence in practical situations. Like the premise of Chaos Theory, many of the choices I faced following the foundation of my childhood experiences produced an unpredictable outcome and a learning opportunity. A critical review of these outcomes has enabled me to put my complex life puzzle together logically, and this coherence has given me many life lessons. I want to share the lessons learned in this coherence process with you in this manuscript.

Taken from the home page of the Glasser Institute's website (Glasser Institute, n.d.), Choice Theory is defined as follows:

Choice Theory® is based on the simple premise that every individual only has the power to control themselves and has limited power to control others. Applying Choice Theory allows one to take responsibility for one's own life and at the same time, withdraw from attempting to direct other people's decisions and lives. Individuals are empowered to take responsibility for their choices and support others in taking ownership of their choices. Negative behaviors reduce in frequency and intensity, relationships strengthen, and satisfaction in life increases.

In this manuscript, I am taking responsibility for my life choices while also providing the reader a contextual framework. As highlighted in the introduction, my goal is to offer you a chance to reflect on my lessons learned from my choices as a husband, father, friend, and employee. What would you have done in the same situation? I readily admit to having made several wrong choices. Recognizing now that I did not have the best childhood and adolescent education, I realize that my emotional and social intelligence was not optimum. The only way to achieve this intelligence would be through interactions with my environment. Each choice I took had both short-term and longer-term results. As I evaluated these results, I was able to discern and adapt behavioral and listening changes necessary to improve my relationships and choices. Some may call this change the development of resilience.

I would like to challenge you to take a few moments and think back on your choices from childhood to the present. Depending on your age, this may be more difficult than you might imagine.

Yet, a critical review of this time will provide an exciting insight into your worldview and innate tendencies. Your childhood sets the stage for the adult you are to become. Doorn, Kamsteeg, and Silberschatz (2019) found significant research exploring the qualitative relationship between one's childhood environment and the resultant adult psychopathology. My review of this educational research suggests that common sense once again prevails. Early traumatic life experiences can carry forward emotional and social insecurities into adulthood (Heim & Nemeroff, 2001); however, Beutel et al. (2017) found that children exhibiting resilience could mitigate many of their early traumatic life experiences. Looking back, I somehow must have developed a resilient nature, which became a defensive trait. So, as you follow my life path, maybe you will see a benefit to developing resilience.

My birth certificate only shows the date of my birth and the names of my parents—no weight, no time of delivery, no footprints or fingerprints, and no physical condition. You would think that this additional information would be of interest to us in the future. On the other hand, it is not like they did not have the information. Was I carried full-term—I seem to remember I was born prematurely? Was I healthy at birth? Could I speak a foreign language? It would be awesome to gain some insight into that particular day, but that information has escaped history. Now, I know that my readers will look at their certificates to see if any vital information is missing. Information-rich birth certificates could offer us essential facts that would benefit us in the future. For example, did this lack of information on my certificate prevent me from gaining a perspective on my earliest challenges? Maybe this information could have explained my resilience against adversity throughout my life.

Growing up, I was a creative and intelligent child with a curious nature about how things worked—to a fault. My way of thinking and processing information was different from other children, and to learn the rules and expectations, I challenged the boundaries. Russert (2017) in his book *Wisdom of Our Fathers,* described his memory of parental roles. He related that the mother was the nurturer, and the father was the disciplinarian (p. 223). As I reflect on my upbringing, I remember the harsh discipline received by my father and grandfather, but I also remember loving relationships with my mother and grandmother. My early childhood aligns with the old English proverb paraphrased as "Children should be seen but not heard." I remember being punished many times for not obeying this rule. I was talkative and wanted to have a conversation with everyone, but this was not allowed. I would have to go to my room while the adults continued their discussions uninterrupted. As a result, I spent a lot of time in my room. I did not realize it then, but these banishments may have been the root cause for my feeling unwanted and restless. Another possibility for my restlessness could have been ADHD or OCD, but these diagnoses were not common in the 1950s.

My childhood was before television, and if my memory serves me correctly, I was about seven years of age before my parents purchased a television. From an epochal perspective, only two channels were available to watch. Television sets were "prized" pieces of wooden furniture, so our television became the centerpiece in the room layout.

Mr. Moose on Captain Kangaroo and Bugs Bunny were my mentors. I loved Mr. Moose and his many manipulative ways of dropping ping pong balls on the Captain, and Bugs Bunny was always tricking Elmer Fudd and Yosemite Sam. Maybe these anthropomorphic animals influenced my behavior, or perhaps their actions resonated with me.

"You are stubborn," my stay-at-home mom would tell me. She also had other ways of expressing her dissatisfaction with my behavior. She had this way of poking her tongue out the side of her mouth to show aggravation. I do not know if you ever watched Tim Allen on the show *Tool Time*; there was an episode when Allen and a man at the hardware store had a rather funny conversation about the female "look," referring to facial expressions. When I watched this episode, I knew what they meant as my mom had mastered the look. She often communicated through her various manifestations, and her tongue expression became very familiar to me. You see, I was that challenging kid who purposely colored outside the lines, and in retrospect, I can now understand why my curious nature and unwelcomed approach to situations frustrated her.

I was a small-framed kid with poor eyesight, and because of my glasses, students would call me "four eyes." Since my creative interests were different from theirs, I became a loner and avoided relationships to protect myself from bullying and ridicule. Still, I was an easy target for name-calling and fights. In elementary and middle school, the guys would bully me constantly, and they would often steal my lunch money when I had some. I think these events may have contributed to my dislike of school, to my social insecurities, and my avoidance of anything but superficial relationships.

My mom was by far the most patient and loving person, and she did not deserve my disruptive demeanor. She did her best to provide for my brother and me, making our clothes, bartering exchanges with other moms, cooking good meals, and making sure we had her support and attention. Like my dad, she also suffered from generational poverty and did not go to college; however, just because we were poor never stopped her from putting her best foot forward. If you met her at church or anywhere outside the house, you would see her well dressed and attractive. She always tried to show a successful appearance outwardly; however, I believe she, like me, had self-esteem issues. I remember a point in her life when she joined an exclusive country club to entertain friends and family. She would dress fashionably during these events, but I can only imagine the insecurities that drove her to take on a high-society appearance. As I was researching pictures and articles for this book, I spoke with a couple who were also charter members at her church, Wesley United Methodist Church in Evans, Georgia. I asked them to recount any fond memories they had about her. The first thing they mentioned was how my mother always was dressed attractively, which made me smile.

At the time, women wore hats and dresses to formal events and church. Once, after church, we went to Clark's Hill, near Augusta, Georgia, to spend the afternoon with Cama and Gagee, the names that I proudly gave to my grandparents. We wanted to retrieve our Boxer dogs, Runt and Penny, who stayed with them during the summer. Mom loved these two animals and was always playing with them at home. Immediately, when Mom stepped from the car, Runt began barking at her hat and would run. No matter how she tried to approach him, he would take off running and bark at her while looking over his shoulder. We all laughed, and the more she tried to get close to him, the funnier the situation became. That day became the family joke for years afterward, and it was fun to see mom also laugh at the memory.

As mentioned above, Cama and Gagee lived at Clark's Hill—the name of the regional area containing a large dam that managed the water flow for the Savannah River. They lived in the first house about half a mile down a dirt road off the main highway. My cousin Tommy and his grandparents lived another half mile down the same street. Their lot abutted the river, and I would go there to dive off their dock and swim. There was a small island about a quarter mile from their dock, and I would swim there to explore the island for lures and arrowheads. Other than our two families and an elderly couple who lived in between them, there were miles of woods and open fields to explore. The dirt road was at least five miles in length, and this road and its several branches all led to the Savannah River. Augusta College and Georgia Railroad Bank later bought the land at the end of this road and developed recreational facilities. The river offered many opportunities for fun and recreation. My dad had a speed boat, and he would pull us on skis and surfboards. I was so fortunate to have had the opportunity to spend my summers with my grandparents and relatives.

Clark's Hill was a utopia. I spent my summers fishing, hunting, exploring, and sometimes I would just lie in the tall grass staring at the cloud formations. There were quail in the fields next to our house, and they frightened me every time a covey would take flight. I would join my cousin Tommy as we searched for fishing lures along the banks of the Savannah River. We would then take these newfound treasures and spend hours trying to catch fish with them.

Tommy was like a brother. We spent many hours together. George and Virginia, Tommy's parents, took a particular interest in our lives. When I visited Tommy at his house, Virginia would make these fantastic meals, and I always looked forward to eating with them. George managed a motel located next to their home, and Tommy and I occasionally provided labor to help repair and improve the facility. As teenagers, we were both interested in electronics, and George helped us start a TV repair business about the time I entered college. Tommy also had loving grandparents. Glenn and Nanny Cadle were inspiring and nurturing, and I enjoyed talking and interacting with them.

At a later date, my dad and Uncle Jim purchased the Clark's Hill house for my grandparents. I was there when they made the presentation. That gift of love was so apparent that I still remember the anticipation and joy of the event even at my young age. I cannot imagine the personal sacrifice required to afford this gift, but the love demonstrated at that moment is indelibly retained in my long-term memory. I can also assure you the gift benefitted me about as much as it did my grandparents. This place was where Gagee taught me how to hunt and fish and where Cama would help me clean and cook my fish and game, even when the game was a small sparrow. Gagee, a retired orderly, would spend hours walking with me through the acres of woods to show me how to listen for rabbits and how to spot squirrels. I was loved and accepted by my grandparents, and I am sure this is why I was so comfortable when I was with them.

A deep chasm approximately a one-half mile wide and seventy-five feet deep was near their house. It was there that I shot my first rabbit. I remember standing on the edge of the chasm looking down when I noticed a rabbit walking through the middle. I aimed my 20-gauge shotgun and nervously pulled the trigger. My shot was accurate, and the rabbit became my first four-legged wild animal to become a meal. My pulse must have been high when I climbed down to get my evening dinner, as I could feel my heart racing in anticipation of getting the rabbit and showing it to Cama.

Cama was the grandma that everyone should have. She would spend evenings scratching my back and telling me stories. She did not mind my curiosity and creativity, and she is probably why I later became a ham radio operator. One afternoon, she brought me some old radios that did not work and asked me to repair them. I spent hours taking them apart to understand how each component worked (this was before the digital age). I wish you could have seen her face when I repaired one of the radios by substituting parts between the radios. She was so proud of me, and I was inspired to find other ways to make her happy.

Cama was also the "mediator" between my mom and my Aunt Rhetta. I never knew what the issue was between them, but Cama would keep them in line, making our Sunday dinners together an enjoyable time. Aunt Rhetta and Uncle Jim were special to me. Rhetta taught me how to throw a baseball, and with this skill, I later became the lead pitcher for my elementary school's little league team. Jim was a mentor, and he used every chance he could to help me understand why a strong work ethic was important. Cama was also a Canasta card shark and loved playing the game with my family and me.

I have heard that all good things must come to an end. Cama was diagnosed with cancer, which is a deadly disease. She was my first experience with death. Looking back, I guess I should have realized that she was dying as she was always in severe pain and seeking assistance for it. I understood what the pastor meant at her funeral when he said she was in a better place. I learned so much from her, and her memory will always bring a smile to my face. I also know her passing upset my parents.

Mom was from Porterdale, Georgia, a small town near Atlanta. She also had a difficult childhood; she was a child of an abusive father. I never learned all of the family dynamics which caused her to spend her teenage years living with her grandparents. I know that she never could end her resentment for her biological father, who I only met once. The town next to Porterdale—Covington, Georgia—was where her family lived. As a child, I always enjoyed visiting them and playing with my cousins.

One cousin, Tim Hay, was the same age as me, and we spent most of our time together exploring their mini-farm and acreage around their house. They had chickens, and we had fun chasing them. Tim was not like me; he was not a risk-taker and always followed the rules. I remember challenging him to cross the road in front of their house with a car approaching. Even though the car was at least a mile away, he would not cross the street because his parents had told him never to go across if he could see a vehicle approaching. I remember running back and forth across the road several times and laughing at him for not crossing. Unfortunately, Tim recently passed away after having a career in the Covington Pharmacy for more than thirty years. My time in Covington was always a great experience as it was so different than my life in Augusta. I must thank my mom for giving me this experience.

My mother lived into her 80s, and my dad passed away at 67—more on my dad later. I remember the day we took mom to live at an assisted living facility and how betrayed she felt. She was a strong woman, and she let me know that she did not want to live with those "old" people. She accused my brother of stealing her money and assets, especially her car. I think she later reconciled that she was wrong, but it took her several years to get to this reconciliation. I should say here that my brother and his wife, Nancye, would have never done anything dishonest, and they were the ones who managed her affairs and health during her final years.

Mom was a devout Christian, and she spent her time at the assisted living facility bringing non-believers to Christ. She continued working for Jesus when she transferred to a nursing home. As I previously mentioned, she was a Charter member for Wesley United Methodist Church in Evans, Georgia, now a mega-church with more than 1,000 members. My mother was one of the founders of the church. She found and negotiated the purchase of a large tract of land where the church now resides. To help start the church, she hosted teas and drop-by events at her home. She was a strong advocate for women in ministry and made several speeches to attract women to the church. As a result, mom became the President of the United Methodist Women's Association. Spirit-led actions characterized her faith, and I am sure my parents are receiving rewards in heaven for their faith and service to the people of Christ.

She loved her grandchildren, and you could see the joy on her face when they came to visit. Now, years after my mother's death, my children still share their special memories of her. I do not doubt that she was a wonderful mom who did her best to raise my brother and me. As I was going through old keepsakes, I found a newspaper article written about her hosting my third birthday, which in detail recounted the party and information on all the attendees. I tried to find the life trajectories of the attendees, and other than my cousin, Tommy Landrum, my social media searches were unsuccessful.

My dad, Robert (Bob) Cadle, suffered from kidney stones and

kidney disease. Incidentally, I have since learned about the impact of diet and fluid intake on our kidneys. In 2017, I spent the Christmas holidays in the hospital due to a large kidney stone blocking my urination ability. My dad received social security benefits for his medical disability. Unfortunately, this benefit did not provide enough support for us, but they tried to make it work. I remember many school days when my lunch consisted of having only a sandwich of two bread slices with mustard in between. Yet, I always had a roof over my head, clothes that fit, and opportunities to play outside.

I clearly remember the screaming and door-slamming episodes that took place during money discussions. I would hide in my room to avoid these highly emotional events. In retrospect, I know my dad must have had internal turmoil over his inability to control our financial situation to provide the support we needed. I believe my parents did the best they could to overcome our financial shortfall; however, being a child from a low-income family established an innate awareness in me of the need for money. I carried this awareness with me into adulthood, and I guess this is one reason that drove me to make sure my children would never experience the stress of being poor. This focus on money possibly pushed me toward immediate gratification rather than learning to pursue longer-term goals.

My dad used the GED approach to finish high school; however, he never attended college. I am not sure if this was regret for him, but I know he valued a college degree, and he pushed me to be the first in our family to earn a degree, which I accomplished. When I was a child, there were few books in our home. The only periodical I remember was our local weekend newspaper that was a source for grocery coupons. Other than in school, I never had anyone read to me or take any interest in my reading. I believe my poor grades in elementary school were a direct result of my reading capability and were possibly the reason for my slow comprehension of the subject matter. Since then, there has been significant educational research in this area, highlighting the need to be reading on grade level by third grade (Annie E. Casey Foundation, 2011). This skill contributes to improved communications and understanding. After I started my different hobbies, I gained insight into how vital reading and discernment are. I learned how to operate Nikon cameras from instruction manuals and assembled radios with the help of circuit diagrams. Today, I enjoy reading (including in foreign languages) to research or gain further knowledge in my areas of interest.

Before my dad's kidney disease would force him to leave the workforce, he managed a SOC service station. He was diligent and worked long hours to make the service station successful. He had a knack for business and understood mechanics, which he had learned from personal experience and his time in the Navy. I remember him making me work at his station. I struggled to do the heavy lifting required to change tires and disassemble car and truck engines. Honestly, I hated the business, and I wanted to do something different to make money. My dad was strict, and expectations for my perfect behavior were evident; however, I constantly failed to meet his expectations. Later in life, I was told he had been extra tough on me because he thought hard manual labor would convince me to pursue a professional (white-collar) career. Well, his strategy worked, as that is precisely the path I followed.

I am grateful for having a father who wanted me to take a different career path than the one he had taken. Unfortunately, his anger issues and disciplinary tactics just pushed me away and made me angry. If I made a mistake, punishment followed. One example that immediately comes to mind is when my dad took me fishing late one evening during the early fall. As a bored nine-year-old, I played with my fishing lure, and it snagged on the lake bottom, which caused the line to break. My dad found this unacceptable, so he made me undress and jump into the water to find and retrieve the lure. This humiliation made me mad, and I was so embarrassed. Maybe this was his idea of a teachable moment, but the lesson I learned was to never go fishing with him again. If only he could have discussed the issues associated with my behavior rather than punishing me, maybe I could have become more self-aware and self-regulated.

My dad's kidney disease put him in the VA hospital for a significant portion of my adolescent years. The doctors finally had to remove one of his kidneys. I do not know if this story is true, but my brother heard from a nurse who was there at that time. She told him the doctors had mistakenly removed the wrong kidney. I do hope this information was not accurate. Dad would stay in the hospital for six to nine-month periods, primarily in isolation. During this time, my relationship with him was to wave at him as he peered out the fifth-floor hospital window. My brother and I played in the magnolia trees around the hospital while our mother visited and checked on him. Later in life, I asked my dad about the experience, and he recounted how he had died on the operating table and lived through an after-death experience. He said that he could see himself hovering above the operating table and then floating toward a beautiful light before he returned to life.

I think that this near-death experience seriously impacted his worldview because he became calmer, more at peace, and a much more relaxed person. My children got to know him after this personality and behavior change, and he became a beloved grandfather. He spent quality time with them and gave each of them unique experiences they still recount today. I am glad their favorable experiences with grandparents were as meaningful as mine.

After recovering from the kidney removal, he eventually was able to return to work. This time, he became an entrepreneur in the auto service business. His long hours and attention to customer need enabled the company to grow, and it finally started paying dividends. He developed a loyal customer base, and on a social level, he was extremely well-liked. Everywhere we went in the Augusta area, people would wave or stop to speak with him. I have often wondered why he did not run for political office.

Years later, after my dad passed away, my brother took over the business. My brother, Joe Cadle, is six years younger, and I believe this age gap put us in different childhood situations. Looking back, I am glad he had more positive childhood experiences than the ones I experienced. Joe was more like my dad and enjoyed doing things with his hands. I do not remember him receiving the types of discipline I had experienced.

Nevertheless, there was one time, which I now regret, that I got him into trouble. Joe and I were playing in the woods not far from home. It was cold, and I chose to start a small fire. The wind was blowing hard and caused the fire to get out of control immediately. A resident called the fire department as the flames were rapidly taking over the wooded area behind houses. The responding firetruck had to jump a ditch—causing significant damage—to reach and squelch the fire. I made Joe agree to lie about how the fire started, and when dad discovered Joe had lied—well, you get the picture.

I now recognize that I missed many good opportunities to be the big brother he was seeking. After my dad's health improved, he was able to work with Joe to expand their auto parts business. I know they gave the company their best effort; however, the competition was fierce, and the company eventually closed. However, I do believe Joe benefitted from dad's entrepreneurial training, as he later started his tire and supply business in Grovetown, Georgia—Gate Two Tire and Supply. His leadership style and attention to detail, coupled with the skills and support of Nancye, his wife, propelled the business forward for more than twenty-five years. They were able to retire after successfully selling the company at the start of 2020.

From my perspective, Joe has been a phenomenal father to his three daughters and a great uncle to my children. You can readily see the love for him in their interactions and conversations. He and

Nancye have lived in one location for most of their married lives, which provided for a stable upbringing for their children. Even though my brother's girls are now grown and married, they still come home for holidays and special events. He also has many close friends, and they have frequent social events. He enjoys a three-acre home on the Savannah River and a vacation home on the ocean near Savannah, Georgia. He and Nancye frequently open their homes to friends and family to share the many fishing, boating, and exploring opportunities these venues offer.

Lessons Learned

As mentioned above, my father appeared to suffer from anger management. Although my dad's anger issues were unfortunate, I have learned to look for the "why" behind behaviors. I now recognize that his battle with kidney disease and financial issues were behind his actions. In addition, I have seen the problems associated with a lack of control over life events. Still, my education has taught me that how you face situations is more about your outlook on life than the situation itself. Everyone experiences setbacks.

My childhood lessons have taught me to try and take the emotions out of crisis and ethical dilemmas. Be slow to respond, and remember that how you use words and power can have lasting effects. Try to find a solution that will "build up" rather than "tear down" relationships.

Remember the golden rule: *do unto others as you would have them do unto you*. This rule is a good reminder of "how" to think. Try to gain an understanding of the motivations of others involved in a conflict. Stephen Covey, the author of *The 7 Habits of Highly Effective People*, said it best: "Seek first to understand, then to be understood." Hold others accountable but be willing to forgive the transgressions and mistakes of others. If possible, give people feedback and offer second chances.

In social situations, I have learned to take the "ABC" approach: A plus B = C, where <u>A</u> is for Awareness, <u>B</u> is for Beliefs, and <u>C</u> is for Courage. Not only do kids say hurtful things, but teenagers and adults also say rude, out-of-character, and inappropriate things. Are you aware of social conversation topics that would annoy you and potentially hurt your feelings? If so, take time to make a list of social comments that could make you angry or spiteful. Next, what are your beliefs that you hold up as your values (honesty, kindness, consistency, work effort, etc.)? Make a list of these beliefs/values. I read that Abe Lincoln had prepared for criticism he might receive while running for public office. A lady once said to him, "Mr. Lincoln, you are two-faced." Lincoln responded, "Ma'am, if I were two-faced, do you think I would be wearing this one?" And this is where the letter C comes in. Lincoln prepared for this criticism. He responded in a way that diffused the situation. By being aware of things that might annoy us and knowing our beliefs, we can respond positively to social remarks that upset us without compromising our values.

Lastly, whether you are or are not a Bible-believing individual, consider reading it. I have learned that the Bible offers many guidelines on moral behavior, forgiveness, and wise choices. There are so many stories that are adaptable to our life situations. Reading the Bible is just one more way to obtain wisdom from those who have gone before us.

I am grateful and blessed to have had two loving parents and grandparents.

CHAPTER 2

Discovering Alpha

We have different gifts, according to the grace given to each of us. If your gift is prophesying, then prophesy in accordance with your faith; if it is serving, then serve; if it is teaching, then teach; if it is to encourage, then give encouragement; if it is giving, then give generously; if it is to lead, do it diligently; if it is to show mercy, do it cheerfully.

—ROMANS 12:6–8

Merriam-Webster provides the following synonyms to define Alpha: baseline, beginning, birth, commencement, dawn, day one, genesis, get-go (also git-go), inception, incipience, incipiency, kickoff, launch, morning, nascence, nascency, onset, outset, start, threshold. I guess any of these words describe my foray into my career.

When I was a teenager, every day was an adventure, an opportunity to explore some new interests that could become a fun thing to do. I remember going under our house to understand how the floors were supported and made. I traced electrical wires from where they entered the house to electrical outlets in the walls, which provided me with a good understanding of how electrical circuits delivered electricity.

The one puzzling gadget was the black box with a rotary dial that would sometimes make a ringing sound to announce someone was trying to speak with us. If you were born in the 1990s or later, you probably do not know this item.

This item was called a telephone, and it was how we had conversations with family, friends, and businesses in our local area. We had yellow phone books to look up the numbers for people and companies. Companies placed advertisements in these phonebooks to help people learn about different products and service offerings. The device's rotary dial allowed the user to dial the phone numbers. Each call went to a local central office where they had telephone operators who received the call and then routed it to the customer. The rotary dial on the apparatus was interesting with its numbers and associated letters. I never researched who designed these dials, but I would love to ask them why no letters accompanied the number one, why the letters, Q and Z, were left off. I was also curious why the number zero came after number nine rather than before the number one. The telephone also had two disconnect buttons that were under the handset. I discovered that you could quickly depress these buttons a select number of times, and these depressions would act the same as if you had dialed the number using the rotary dial.

Once I was home alone, I decided to disassemble our telephone to learn how the different components enabled the dial tone sound and the bell to ring. I remember taking the phone apart, starting with the outside shell and then removing several wire connections. Then it dawned on me that I might not be able to reassemble the device. So you can imagine the panic I felt when I heard my mother open the back door. Fortunately for me, it went back together quickly and worked, so no one ever knew what I had done—whew!

As recounted in Chapter One, school days were dull, and my grades were barely passing. In the seventh grade, the only class I enjoyed was science. My teacher learned of my endeavors with the telephone and my curiosity about engineering and technology. He allowed me to use class time to diagnose and repair non-working radios and televisions that he would often bring into class. He would send me to the library to find schematics and books on electronics that might provide me with insight into troubleshooting and repairing these items. During one of these library visits, I found a schematic and manual on the rotary telephone that had mystified me. The telephony manuals explained how the phone, and the transmission poles, wires, transformers, and central office connected to the network. Cell phones have changed the way telecommunications take place in today's economy. Software, rather than people, now runs these networks and call connections. According to one Internet report, more than 100,000 switchboard operators lost their jobs due to digital technologies.

While gathering additional information on telephony communications, I noticed a copy of the "QST" magazine, the official magazine of the American Amateur Radio League for Amateur (Ham) radio. The magazine was fascinating and piqued my interest. As I read the magazine, I discovered that hams could build their transmitters, receivers, and antennas, enabling them to contact other hams around the world wirelessly. I also learned that to become a ham, a Federal Communications Commission radio theory and Morse code test were required to obtain a license to operate in specific frequency allocations. These license categories were Novice (beginner), Technician, General, Advanced, and Amateur Extra Class.

I became obsessed with getting a ham license and studied Morse code and radio theory until I was ready for my test. I joined the Amateur Radio Club of Augusta, and they provided me with a receiver to use for Morse code comprehension. I passed the Novice test and received my license (call sign WN4AZX). I later progressed up to Advanced (call sign WB4EMV), which I still have today, approaching sixty years later. After receiving my license, I ordered a Knight Kit T-60 transmitter kit and spent many hours putting the kit together. I spent hours in the library to study antenna configurations and used this knowledge to build and install a dipole antenna for the forty-meter band.

My grades in high school still reflected my dislike for school, but they were better than the grades in middle school. The significant change in high school was my problem-solving ability and different ways of thinking, which caught the attention of an ROTC instructor. I questioned his approach to a project and explained a better way to proceed. He wanted a student with a curious and confident nature who could communicate with diverse students with different backgrounds and interests. The success with this project led to being promoted to Major and serving as Battalion Commander. The diversity, the challenge, the personal demands, and the importance of the position pushed me to become a leader and advocate for my Battalion. The opportunity helped me with my insecurities, and, due to my rank, I became well known to the students, which enabled me to improve my social interactions.

There were many things I wanted as a teenager. I was interested in photography and wanted to obtain Nikon gear. These cameras were known for offering the best picture quality. Ham radio was also a fun hobby, and I wanted to purchase equipment that could expand my ability to work DX (ham lingo for distance stations). Since my family could not give me money for these items, I cut lawns and landed a job at Augusta Radio Company. I sold records and transistor radios and assisted our repair technician when times were slow up front. I quickly added value to the backroom technical function. My knowledge gained from the repair bench enabled me to begin selling the store's expensive home entertainment systems, which produced most of the store's revenues. I was so successful selling the stereo equipment that he started paying me a dollar for each $1,000 system

I sold. As I look back to this time, I do not believe that this was a fair deal. What do you think?

My nonconformist attitude and strong interest in electronics seemed to resonate with the store's technician, Mr. Neal Jewett. Neal was seven years older than me. Like me, he was a ham operator, and each day working with him was fun and a learning experience. He told me about the horrors of the Vietnam War, and I believe that his reflective stories were behind why I later chose the Army Reserve rather than active duty. Neal became the big brother I never had, and although we enjoyed our time together, I should state here that my emotional maturity was not advanced enough to know when to disagree with him or say no.

We were on our way home from a South Carolina assignment when Neal decided to stop and grab a few ears of corn from a corn field that we were passing. After several minutes, he returned to the car with his planned supper. I was the get-away driver and started to pull away from the field. Just at that moment, a car pulled in front of us and stopped. The driver jumped out with a shotgun and yelled for us to get out of the vehicle. As Neal stepped out, the man hit him with the butt of the gun. I was terrified as he held his gun on us while waiting for the police to arrive. After the police arrived, we went to the station. We were later released and warned about the seriousness of stealing—a lesson that left an indelible mark in my memory. As I finished writing this paragraph, I looked up Mr. Jewett on the Internet to learn that he went on to become a biomedical engineer and retired from a local hospital after twenty years of service. I noticed that he passed in 2008, and the fond memories of our time together, including the time he bought me my first beer, made me smile and remember the quantity and quality of time he invested in me.

That beer brings back some funny memories. One day after working late, we went next door to a bar and joined several of Neal's friends. I was going to order a coke when the bartender put a beer in front of me. I do not believe anyone at the table realized that this would be my first time having an alcoholic drink. As I took several sips, my mind tried to figure if I was drunk. The more I thought about it, the desire to leave and walk home (I lived nearby) became my driving thought process. Anyway, about halfway through the glass of beer, I told the group that I needed to leave—I do not remember the reason. As I walked home, I could feel my heart racing, and I kept taking inventory of how I felt. Of course, I was fine, but I was so afraid my dad would find out that I had been drinking and would give me another one of those dreaded spankings. It is too bad that this incident did not establish a guardrail relative to drinking alcohol. Since that date, I have had a few experiences with sometimes drinking too much, but I am glad to say that I have no dependence on alcohol of any kind as of this writing.

I met my boss's expectations at Augusta Radio; however, I started looking around for opportunities that offered higher compensation. I later decided to leave Augusta Radio and become a salesman at a large department store working in appliances. I successfully closed sales, but it bothered me that my boss appeared to have a real problem with ethics. After my jail experience for stealing corn from a cornfield, I never wanted to risk doing something illegal. The store was running a sales promotion during the summer. My boss placed an air conditioner atop a large block of ice, and the person who correctly guessed the time and date that the ice melted, causing the air conditioner to touch the ground, would win. People would place their names and guesses on a clipboard near our sales desk. Finally, the contest sign-up period ended. My boss then waited until the store closed and then used a hairdryer to melt the ice, resulting in no one winning the air conditioner. After that event, I decided to move on to another opportunity.

I took a commission-only job with J.M. Fields. My electronics experience provided me with a depth of knowledge about electronic equipment, enabling me to quickly learn the store's electronics and appliance products and how best to present their features to customers. I became a fantastic salesman, making significant commissions ($300 per week) quickly after joining the department. My savings account was quickly expanding, and I had saved nearly $2,000 in just a few weeks. As I reflected on my employment with J.M. Fields, I remember asking Elaine, my future wife, to marry me in their parking lot under one of their bright lights. I was so romantic—ha, ha.

I was not a fan of school, and college was no different. To this day, I remember overhearing the college counselor telling my dad I was not college material and suggesting that dad should consider putting me in a trade school. I know this hurt him to hear, but my overhearing this instilled a drive in me to prove the counselor wrong. As a result, I was able to get into Augusta College on probation. My probationary period was two quarters, and by the end of this time, I had to demonstrate that I could pass college-level coursework. I took relatively easy classes and was able to get the required "C" for admission; however, as the coursework became more demanding, I was unable to continue with passing grades. I failed calculus and chemistry and barely achieved passing grades in my other classes. I knew something must change, but I struggled with this decision. I was blessed and grateful to receive funding for my tuition from the Exchange Club of Augusta, but I still had to earn money to buy books and other items needed for my classes.

Then I discovered the college's billiards room. I became excellent at billiards, and there were few times when I lost a game. Once, the college invited a well-known pool shark to our campus, and I had the opportunity to play with him. Knowing that I had this seemingly once-in-a-lifetime chance to win, I spent hours practicing. Finally, as the underdog, I had the opportunity to start the game. I broke the balls and ran the table down to the "eight" ball, the ball I had to sink to win. It was lined up almost straight with a corner pocket, and I am sure you guessed it; I was so nervous that I missed the final shot allowing him to win the game.

My college classes demanded significant study time to keep my grades in the passing range. I tried study groups; however, these students spent more time discussing their interests and politics than the subject matter. They talked about the Martin Luther King and Robert Kennedy assassinations, the Vietnam War, and several other events taking place at that time. They constantly discussed their interest in attending Woodstock, outside of Bethel, New York. If you have not heard of Woodstock, make sure you look into why 400,000 kids went there in 1969.

The Vietnam war was escalating, and our government issued a mandatory draft based on your birth date. My draft number was fifty, so I immediately applied for and received a student deferment; however, remembering Mr. Jewett's stories, I joined the U.S. Army Reserve in 1970.

Benefitting from my ROTC experience, the Army promoted me to Private First Class (E-3) and placed me in their medical unit. Once again, my electronics experience proved valuable, and after basic training, my reserve unit allowed me to teach electronics during my annual two-week active-duty requirement.

I became a 91A10 Medical Specialist and spent significant time with doctors and nurses to work with patients and further my medical education, which, believe it or not, I enjoyed. Nevertheless, I will never forget my basic training experience. I arrived at Fort Polk, Lousiana, when the North Vietnamese soldiers and the U.S. soldiers were going through a significant confrontation. Fort Polk was known for housing German prisoners during WWII and as an advanced infantry training facility during the Vietnam War. Because of the similar environmental conditions to Southeast Asia, this Army Post was where soldiers received their battle training before being sent to combat. My disdain for structure and routines caused me to risk receiving an Article 92(1) violation by the drill sergeants. Now, I must admit that some of these sergeants had more drill skills than intellectual skills. For example, one day, I challenged a sergeant to a one-arm pushup contest in front of my squad. I remember doing seventy pushups with my right arm and sixty more with my left. My challenger could only do twenty, and he was so mad that he decided to report me. He asked me for my name, and I pointed at my shirt and spelled U S A R M Y. He wrote this down and stormed off to the officers' building to report me.

Later he found me and informed me that my punishment would be to guard a nail that he had earlier nailed into a tree. That night after he left me at my post, I removed the nail and took it with me to the beer joint I frequented. A short time later, the sergeant stormed in and started yelling at me for leaving my post. I reminded him that my job was to guard the nail, and I wish you could have seen his face when I pulled the nail from my pocket. Little did I know at the time that my disrespectful antics could get me killed.

One evening, we had the task of low crawling under barbed wire, while at the same time, machines fired tracer bullets above us. When I was about halfway, bullets started hitting all around me. Immediately the lights came on, and the speaker blurted out orders to remain still. Not me; I probably finished that task in the fastest time ever recorded. Many of my fellow soldiers believed that the event was not an accident. After this incident, I was ready to return home and start the next phase of my life.

Lessons Learned

Alpha for me was my childhood and the events above. Although my interests were in technology and engineering, my dad wanted me to pursue a BBA degree in accounting and finance. Although my coursework has been extremely valuable in my career endeavors, I wonder how life would have turned out if I had pursued a technology degree—my advice: do not impose your aspirations on children. Instead, watch them and interact with them to discover each child's unique gifts. Above all, give your children a voice and give them positive and constructive reinforcement.

CHAPTER 3

A Career Begins

*May the favor of the Lord our God rest on us; establish the
work of our hands for us—yes, establish the work of our hands.*

—Psalm 90:17

My goal for the next section of this book is to highlight impactful career endeavors and a pattern of conflict. Work has always been about the challenge and the opportunity to learn something new and valuable. One might say that each career move was a chance to expand my knowledge and gain experience. Although each option began well, many of my career endeavors ended early due to my inability to confront conflict and my constant search for a better job opportunity. I believe these tendencies created restlessness as I sought to control each situation. My learned defense mechanisms and lack of emotional intelligence would play a role in most of my early career choices.

Roberts Furniture Company

Roberts Furniture Company was my first real job. I applied to become their warehouse manager, responsible for inventory, receiving, and delivery. After getting hired, I had three direct reports which were responsible for post-sale deliveries. I quickly learned how to unload trucks with heavy furniture and bedding by myself. I remember standing up king-size mattresses and balancing them on the middle of my back. I would then walk them over to their inventory location and put them in stacks of eight. Over several months working in the warehouse, I became knowledgeable of how furniture was constructed, allowing me to become proficient with minor repairs. This knowledge also enabled me to give the sales staff training seminars for any new line of furniture that we were introducing.

After a year of working in this capacity, I moved to the sales floor. There I learned how to use targeted questions to zero in on a customer's interests and guide them in decision making. I quickly became the number two sales leader out of five sales associates. In some months, I captured the number one spot. However, the top salesman had a name that everyone recognized, Hoot Gibson (an American rodeo champion and film star). He would engage customers through life stories enabling him to capture their attention long enough to sell our furniture. I learned the art of storytelling and used this skill to add significant commissions to my base salary. I was successful at selling bedding and bedroom suites. As I write this, I recall my lightbulb experience.

A Beautyrest mattress representative had presented the selling features for their line of mattresses. He was a hefty gentleman and wanted to show us how to use a lightbulb to sell Beautyrest mattresses. He placed the lightbulb between the mattress and the box spring and then jumped onto the area. Most people would expect to see the lightbulb burst; however, it survived, and he told us to let customers know this was just an example of how well the mattress conformed to the human body. Honestly, I could not wait to demonstrate this sales strategy to a customer. Within the next couple of days, I had my chance. I took my customer up to the second floor to our bedding section and proceeded to place the lightbulb under the mattress. I then jumped onto the bed and cringed as I heard the lightbulb explode. The lightbulb bursting was apparent from anywhere in the store. Fortunately, I had learned to turn any negative situation into a positive one. When I raised the mattress showing the fractured lightbulb, I turned to my customer and said, "This is a Beautyrest. If this had been another mattress, the burst of the lightbulb would have ripped the cover." My customer agreed and purchased the mattress set.

I quickly learned the system for furniture operations and recognized the system components: sales and inventory, finance, operations, and accounting. My coursework at Augusta College enhanced my knowledge of finance and accounting, but I regrettably had not taken any management or leadership courses.

The headquarters for Robert's Furniture was in North Carolina. My boss, who was about my age, told me our chain of furniture stores was expanding and that he had introduced me as a potential store manager. He valued my knowledge and experiences and felt that I would be a perfect manager for one of their new stores. He arranged an interview, and I was ready to tell the recruiter how much I knew about the company's business operations. My leadership training consisted of shadowing my boss. Each morning he would meet with the employees and tell them their duties for that day, and then he would go outside and smoke a cigar. When the recruiter asked me to explain how to lead a store's operations, I let him know the importance of instructing employees on daily duties and smoking cigars outside, just like I had learned from my boss. Yes, I said that. Later that day, the recruiter let my boss know that I was no longer a candidate for a new store in another geographical area. My boss's feedback about my interview mistakes let me know that my future opportunities in the store chain would be limited to sales. Hearing this, I chose to seek other options. The store manager interview demonstrated my potential and let me know that I needed more leadership experience to improve my career trajectory.

Friedman Jewelers

I interviewed at several companies before landing a job as the internal auditor for Friedman Jewelers, a regional jewelry chain. After completing months of store audits, my insight into individual stores was exceptional. I created charts that became our dashboard for sales, charge-offs, employee turnover, cost of sales, and inventory overages/shortages. This dashboard became the guide that determined which of our forty stores I would audit.

I became the company's forensic auditor and discovered several fraudulent activities by store managers. For example, I noticed that one store manager took wedding rings out of inventory under a loan category. The odd thing was that he would take the loaned item over a weekend and return it the following Monday. With some targeted questions, I learned that he used the ring to propose to a girl, which offered him some romantic opportunities. However, he would then tell the girl that he had to get the ring sized for her. Then, after a few days, he would break up with her. Naturally, these antics did not go over well with management, leading to his termination.

I also discovered a ruse by one of our corporate leaders. He had a collection presentation where he presented new collection agents a story about the high accounts receivable charge-off percentage before joining the company. He explained that since joining the organization, the charge-off percentage lessened significantly. However, he failed to tell everyone that when he joined Friedmans, he convinced management to write off all the delinquent receivables aged over ninety days. You can imagine his surprise when I pointed this out to him in front of the collection agents. However, this opportunity to show my knowledge did not end well. The VP let my boss know what I had done, and he reprimanded me for my actions. He told me never to criticize anyone in front of others, a good lesson for me to learn.

Besides my forensic skills, I was adept with technology implementation as many manual financial functions were to be automated, and I was the key person responsible for automating the processes. The leadership of Friedman's recognized this and asked me to set up the point-of-sale system in a new division of Friedmans called Key Wholesale. I did so well in my duties that I received a promotion to Assistant Controller; however, even though my responsibilities substantially increased, my compensation remained the same. So once again, I chose to seek other opportunities.

First Railroad and Banking Company

I responded to an ad in the newspaper for a banking management position. My interview went so well that I took the position as the Accounting Manager for Georgia Railroad Bank and Trust Company of Georgia, a $300 million bank. In this role, I would be responsible for leading a team that consolidated the accounting operations of forty-one internal departments. My team also updated the "manual" general ledger, and I prepared/filed the bank's shares tax return. As I reflect on my first few days in this new position, I recognize that I should have postponed my start as I had the flu and felt terrible; however, I knew how much I would miss if I stayed at home until I was feeling better. Therefore, I took cold medications and did my best not to infect anyone else. The job was challenging but not as difficult as navigating the political environment.

I quickly learned that your title and the square footage of your office seemed to be equally as important as compensation. Newly appointed Vice Presidents would measure the size of their new office to determine if it corresponded to their position expectations. My peer associate was the Manager of Financial Reporting. He had been in his position for some time, and I could tell he resented my being there. I surmised that he had wanted my role to become a direct report to him. We had personality issues from day one, and he started insulting me in conjunction with providing me little support. In addition, he had a colleague who played along with his game of demeaning insults, which challenged my motivation for working at the bank. As I was working on this manuscript, I took a moment to discover what had happened with him later in his career. I found a press release announcing his retirement as CEO of a local credit union. As I read the announcement, I could not help but laugh out loud as I read his statement saying that he had learned an organization's most important asset was its people. "At the end of the day, nothing is more important than people. I always knew that, but I didn't fully understand it until I got here." I wish he had realized this when we worked together.

Fortunately, Mr. Fleming Love, the SVP of the bank's holding company, liked me and valued my work contribution. My unique task focus was what he needed, and I made sure that my work met or exceeded his expectations. The more time I spent with him, the less my colleagues' insults mattered. I enjoyed my duties and responded quickly to Mr. Love's requests for information. I had the opportunity to work with him on a tax matter that could save the bank millions of dollars. The amount of the bank's equity capital determined the state taxes that were due. I suggested that the bank receive a credit against their capital for the amount of foreclosed property as this was an unplanned use of capital. If we were successful in deducting foreclosed property, these amounts would exceed the bank's equity, and we would not owe any state income tax. We made this case in court and prevailed, thereby saving the bank the anticipated assessments.

In 1978, the holding company for Georgia Railroad Bank (First Railroad and Banking Company) had several open tax years under audit, ownership in the Georgia Railroad train infrastructure, and an aggressive effort to acquire new banks. My relationship with Mr. Love continued to develop, and he championed my promotion to accounting officer to the First Railroad Board of Directors, which they approved. Wow, my new position was like drinking from a firehose as I now had financial oversight for a leasing company, a mortgage company, and a commercial paper operation. My duties also consisted of the monthly financial consolidation of eight banks, the Federal Tax Return, and helping Mr. Love with the open tax year audits. At the time of the promotion, I was also running for President of Georgia Railroad Bank and Trust's 450-employee social club. I won the election, and this was a confidence builder. I am sure the opportunity to plan social events for the bank's employees would have been fun; however, I declined to accept the election results due to the demands of my new accounting officer position.

First Railroad's Controller became ill, and I took the role of acting controller. This change in responsibilities was a new challenge that excited me. Unfortunately, Mr. Love had his rivals, which led to internal spats and arguments unbecoming of grown men. In the end, his opposition was able to convince the Board to hire an outside CPA (I did not become a CPA until later in my career) to become Controller. While working at First Railroad, I became friends with external audit partners. I took the chance to share with them my disappointment about not being promoted to controller. They understood and mentioned an opportunity to become the Chief

Financial Officer for a finance company in Alpharetta, Georgia. Not receiving the promotion to the Controller position pushed me to pursue this new opportunity. I do look back and wonder if I had approached the situation differently and talked out my concerns. Maybe I would have gained a different perspective and continued my employment. Serving as Assistant Controller for a billion-dollar bank would not have been a bad thing to have on my resume.

International Marketing Services

My next endeavor was a significant shift from the banking culture. I went from a traditional suit culture to a culture of jeans and informality. My new company, International Marketing Services (IMS), included a finance company and an extensive quarter horse breeding and sales operation. The majority owner, Mr. Vic Matthews, was of Greek heritage and had immigrated from Australia. He had traveled extensively and enjoyed conversing about different cultures. My extensive cultural knowledge of various countries obtained from my ham radio experience enabled Vic and me to become friends quickly.

It was easy for me to see that the finance company profits funded the quarter horse operation, thereby providing Mr. Matthews with significant tax benefits while at the same time allowing him to enjoy his horse lifestyle. In addition to my accounting duties, he added the responsibility of establishing credit lines for the finance company and helping him accomplish some other personal interests. I developed a financial package that would support the growth in IMS's accounts-receivable. A line of credit would give us the time necessary to allow accounts receivable cash flows to exceed interest and principal payments. I presented the package to several banks and finance companies. My efforts were successful, and GE Capital provided us with a $12 million line of credit. The line allowed us to draw down 80 percent of each new account receivable amount, which enabled us to fund our cash flow needs and provide additional funds for special projects.

Mr. Matthews had a special father-like relationship with each of his key people, but he also knew how to play us against each other. Again, like at the bank, my peers and I had a discordant relationship. Again, I was the outsider who seemed to threaten their close relationship with Vic. Also, like the bank, these individuals had worked for IMS for years to obtain their senior positions, and they accordingly resented my entry at a senior level.

The banking positions had taught me to focus my energies on the work and ensure that my output exceeded expectations. Under-promise and over-deliver became my motto. If only I had engaged my counterparts on an emotional and personal level to explore and resolve conflicts, it would not have appeared as if I were trying to lessen their importance to the organization. Unfortunately, my childhood upbringing never taught me emotional intelligence, which, now as I look back, I can understand why I have struggled in every job with personal relationships and communications. As I continued to become a valued asset to the owner, my salary quickly became more than three times what I made at the bank, and I was given a new Jaguar XK-6 Vanden Plas Sedan as a company car. At thirty years of age, coming from my background, I felt as though I had conquered my quest for success. Little did I know that my success would again lead to ethical conflicts.

Vic and I built a wine vault that would hold 4,000 bottles of wine, and we proceeded to buy fine wines, cases at a time, to fill up the cooler. We hoped that these investments would grow in value over the next few years. In addition, we obtained books on fine wines and participated in many wine tastings to develop our expertise. Our wine vault primarily contained red wines from all over the world.

Our attempt to develop sophisticated palates also involved expanding our vocabulary of wine terminology. We would speak about each wine's body, aroma, character, and taste and then log our findings.

During this time, Vic granted me 1.3 percent of the company's equity, which I calculated to be worth approximately $150,000. He then asked me to design an expansion for the corporate headquarters and to oversee the project. I was intrinsically and extrinsically motivated to do an excellent job for him and the company. In addition, he challenged me to start a travel agency in Denver, Colorado, to capitalize on the travel costs of our Denver-based sales organization. My funny story here is that I had to determine a strategy that would enable us to enter the market quickly. I performed research on the Denver market and learned approximately 200 travel companies were competing for business in the area. Upon further examination, I discovered that the average salary for a senior sales agent was $28,000. The next day, I ran a newspaper ad announcing that my new agency, Trademark Travel, sought to hire experienced agents at a beginning salary of $31,000. Within a month, I recruited five agents that brought a significant amount of business with them. After only a month in operation, we were on track to make $1.4 million in annual revenue.

Then, just as I was making progress with the construction project, the travel agency, and my peer relationships, a significant event happened. For a while, I had observed that Vic and his wife were having some personal disagreements and conflict, but I never expected that their marital relationship would enter divorce proceedings. I had a respectful and friend-like relationship with both individuals, and I knew this breakup would pull on my heartstrings and possibly harm my job. However, almost immediately after learning of the separation, my concerns materialized. When Vic's job responsibilities required him to travel for extended periods, I served as his intermediary to handle the legal proceedings. This duty challenged my integrity, and I subsequently had a frank discussion with Vic that brought me to tears. Unfortunately, that discussion was the beginning of the end of our relationship. Yet, I will never forget several humorous stories during my tenure with International Marketing Services.

As a shareholder, I could take bottles of wine home to use in entertaining. Although I had become an oenophile, I had not shared my knowledge of wine with Elaine. One day, I came home after work to see a 1962 bottle of Chateau Laffite Rothschild open and sitting on the kitchen counter. Why was this $700 bottle of wine opened? Was there a get-together I might have forgotten? At that moment, Elaine, my lovely wife, entered the kitchen, so I asked her about it. She told me that she needed a bottle of wine to make wine spritzers. At that moment, I realized that I had never shared the value of the different wines I had stored in our wine cooler; whoops, this was a memorable lesson! Another story I fondly remember is about Elaine's interest in one of the farm's quarter horses. The horse had all the characteristics of a champion with its gentle nature, muscular profile, and beautiful color. The horse was ready for the upcoming auction; however, I wanted to purchase it for Elaine. I had the chance to pre-buy the horse for $30,000 if I agreed to let the horse go through the auction. My price would be the minimum bid, and the horse would not sell below the minimum bid. If the auction brought in more than this amount, I had the opportunity to pocket the difference. I could not bring myself to risk $30,000 on this horse, so I chose to pass on the offer. The next day the horse went through auction, and the winning bid was $250,000. Well, maybe this was not such a humorous story.

Software Concepts

Between 1986 and 1988, I worked for Software Concepts in Atlanta, Georgia. My introduction to the founding partners of the company was through my Deloitte auditor friends. They suggested that I would be an excellent choice to become their Controller. The software company had grown to six million dollars in revenue, and they were exploring new business opportunities. They needed someone who could guide them in decision-making and help them align resources to goals. I decided to take the position, which paid a similar amount to my earnings at International Marketing Services. The company developed software that served as the intelligence in carpet cutting processes. Their client carpet company personnel would just enter the dimensions of the customer requirements, and our intelligence software would run the machines. The best way I can think to describe this is to think of it as the early use of artificial intelligence and robotics. I quickly implemented the Financial Accounting Standards Board guideline for software providers and updated their payables and collections procedures. The company executives appreciated my work ethic, and for a while, we had a great relationship.

One condition of my employment was that I obtain my certification in public accounting. I had recently taken the exam but had not received the test results. My earlier career experiences fulfilled the experience requirement, so I only needed to pass the CPA exam to become certified. Every few days, the President would stop by my office and inquire about my exam, and not knowing the answer, I would assure him that he would be the first person I would notify when my grades came in. I called the State Board of Accountancy to inquire as to when I should receive my grades. The examiner told me the grades went out several weeks earlier. I had not received my grades as puzzling, and on further investigation, she found a problem with my mailing address. Due to my feeling nervous before the exam began, I left off my address house number on the test result notification card. I provided them the missing information, but the lady still would not tell me my grades; however, she hinted

I should not worry. Several days later, I finally received my passing scores, letting me know that I was now a Certified Public Accountant. I was glad this situation had come to a positive conclusion, yet the stress involved impacted my emotions.

Now, after meeting all the qualifications for the job and establishing a professional relationship with the founders, I came in one day to find the two founders at odds with each other. Their disagreement was so profound that they were looking for ways to reach a buy/sell agreement between them. To make matters worse, they each tried to convince me to support their takeover of the company. After realizing that any reconciliation was impossible, I suggested that they consider selling the company or finding a merger partner, to which they agreed. The next few months were stressful, but I could negotiate a sale to another software provider and received a one-year salary bonus for leading the transaction. I declined an offer to become the assistant controller for the acquiring company and called my accounting friends to assist me in looking for my next career endeavor. Honestly, I was glad the Software Concepts experience was now behind me.

Lessons Learned

At this point, maybe I should highlight some observations. First, quitting a job is both a choice and a chance to use what you have learned to enhance success in your next endeavor. However, the objective observation for me is that I did not have a long-term career plan. Do you have one? I could have used my banking and finance skills to advance my career within the financial industry; however, this never occurred. Hopefully, if you are following a similar path, you will stop and re-evaluate your career goals.

When you evaluate and consider a job change, stop and look at both the benefits and the potential pitfalls. Ask questions like:

Why is the position vacant?

How is the culture in this new organization?

How will this position build on my past work experience?

What new experience or learning opportunity will this new position offer?

Try and look beyond the inducement for the change and determine if the change aligns with your career goals.

CHAPTER 4

Achieving Self-Efficacy

When I was a child, I talked like a child, I thought like a child, I reasoned like a child. When I became a man, I put the ways of childhood behind me.

—1 Corinthians 3: 11

hile writing about my career changes, you may have noticed certain traits emerging—some good and some needing improvement. I had a strong work ethic, a benefit I received from my father; however, I must have felt the emotional need to obtain approval for my skills and knowledge in each career position. My focus on tasks took precedence over forming personal relationships. At the time, I did not realize that my social intelligence could be one reason for my frequent job changes. My constant development of a plan B in anticipation of jobs not working out may have resulted from my social awkwardness. However, as I developed a sense of self-reliance, I began to explore intrinsic tendencies that tended to make me more resilient and confident in my abilities.

As each opportunity provided new experiences, I became adept at evaluating an organization by applying a 360-degree analysis.

I quickly discerned if an organization's potential aligned with its operations by looking at industry trends, competitive forces, internal strengths and weaknesses (SWOT analysis), staff alignment and accountability, and financial statements. This analysis enabled me to suggest strategic improvements, and each time they were implemented, they were successful. Of course, I tried to be impartial in this analysis by keeping my perceptions to a minimum.

There is significant research on meta-perceptions, i.e., relating how a person's self-view influences his or her worldview. Maybe my early self-esteem and distrust issues pushed me to become task-focused over learning the emotional and social skills needed to be well-rounded. I perceived that excelling in tasks was the most crucial success attribute to career growth. This task focus allowed me to excel in business while not having to be challenged with people interactions. I am glad that I began to understand that leadership was as much about trust as subject-matter knowledge. Unfortunately, my social intelligence may have kept me from pursuing growth in other opportunities. I learned in my next position to take social risks by forcing myself to listen actively and becoming more open and empathetic.

This new knowledge and commitment enabled me also to improve my family relationships. I missed cues from my wife relating to my work travel requirements and how our several relocations impacted her. I had taken her away from her parents, siblings, and grandparents, and friends. I do regret not realizing earlier the impact these changes must have had on her. The lesson I have learned is to never take anyone for granted, especially family members, and to be open to candid conversations, even if they may threaten your self-esteem. In addition, you can learn from constructive criticism. Taking chances involves risk, but from risk can come reward. I believe these revelations enabled me to excel in my future career endeavors.

Solid State Systems/Alcatel

My friends at the accounting firm continued to be helpful in career searches. I let them know what had transpired, and they immediately introduced me to the CEO of Solid State Systems, a telecom manufacturer specializing in automatic call distribution systems (ACDs). These were the automated systems that immediately route your in-coming call to a telemarketing agent with the personal and profile information associated with your telephone number. The receiving agent would use this information to personalize sales and service presentations. The uses for this type of system are many. For example, E-911 calls automate location identification, type of caller (company, residential, or mobile), and personal/profile information associated with the call and then route the call to specific agents or officers. With the advent of the Internet of Things, ACDs allow devices to call your cell phone for service notification. Other applications are so forward-thinking that clothes can monitor respiration, pulse, and distress signs for police or service personnel. An interactive voice response call is automatically placed to the distressed individual to confirm health status if a problem occurs. Depending on the person's health status, a distress call might go out to an ambulance service. ACDs enable these types of applications and uses.

My ham radio experience was relatable to Solid State's operations. In addition, the fact that I could read a circuit diagram, understand telephony systems, and offer significant banking and finance expertise made me a great candidate for their CFO search. After my interview with the CEO and his leadership team, I landed the job. I chose to leave Software Concepts to enter the telephone manufacturing industry. Leaving my job was not an easy choice. When I told my superior my plans to leave, he offered me the opportunity to become their global marketing director. Though the offer was tempting, the chance to work closer to home and lessen my travel requirements tipped the decision scale toward Solid State Systems.

In our first meeting, the CEO disclosed to me that Solid State was in financial trouble. The owners had used the manufacturing business as the income threshold needed to buy the building and acreage alongside Interstate 400. Two unexpected events happened concurrently. First, AT&T was the primary buyer for the company's products and sold the ACD switches to telemarketing companies; however, due to recent federal legislation introducing competition into this industry, Solid State lost their exclusive arrangement with AT&T's Regional Bell Operating Companies (RBOCs). The legislation required the breakup of the Bell System, and this divestiture harmed the company. Second, the divestiture required Solid State to form new customer relationships with each of the divested RBOCs or to set up new distributorships. Solid State's management, in my opinion, made a strategic error. Rather than building from the success and relationship with AT&T, they chose to form new distributorships that would compete with the RBOCs for end-user customers.

The CEO asked me to structure a sale or merger of the company and do it quickly before sales and cash reserves declined. He was in communication with National Telecommunications, PLC (NT) out of London, and he advised me to analyze the benefits/risks of a transaction with them. My due diligence discovered that NT had a small switch that could add to our product line and enable us to reach new customers. This opportunity was my first experience doing a transaction in a foreign country, and I was ready to get to work. The NT Representative was a senior financial person with a Cockney British accent. My attempt to understand his dialect was a significant challenge, but I became accustomed to his language structure and cultural differences over time. I was able to work closely with NT to complete a merger on October 7, 1988. Then, shortly after the merger, another unexpected situation arose.

I learned that NT had a chance to sell their company to Alcatel, which they successfully pursued. Since we were a recent merger with NT, we became a subsidiary of Alcatel, one of the largest telecom companies in the world. Alcatel was a French firm, and fortunately for me, I had studied French in school. Solid State's CEO let me know that a group of Alcatel executives would be coming soon and wanted me to present the financial side of our business to them. I surmised this upcoming meeting might be stressful to Solid State's founders, as the acquisition by Alcatel was unexpected. After the NT/Alcatel transaction was closed, I began to see red flags. The executive team had several closed-door meetings without me. As you may imagine, this was worrisome to me, and I suspected something was amiss.

I then heard from our NT Controller that the Alcatel team would be arriving the following week, but I heard nothing about this from the Solid Stare executives. Additionally, he told me what the team would be expecting to see. He suggested that I put together a notebook containing all the critical information about our business, including my thoughts on expanding our operations and sales. I worked long hours on the notebook and completed it just in time for their arrival the next day. I made a copy for our CEO, but I left it on his desk since he was not there.

I knew the hotel where our guests would be staying, so I reached out to them to suggest that we meet early to go over my notebook information. I suggested that this information may aid them in getting a quick understanding of our business before visiting the facility. They agreed! We met for breakfast and went through the book in detail.

My French classes in college paid off. The Alcatel team primarily conversed among themselves in French. I could tell they were highly impressed and happy with the information I was providing them. When we finished going through the notebook, I was assigned to work with their financial guy and give him a facility tour. The rest of the Alcatel team met with the Solid State executive team. I received an invitation to join the team for a drink later that evening at their hotel.

Due to how the day progressed, my CEO and I never had time to discuss the day's activities. Although I assumed termination might be on the agenda, I was still looking forward to our evening meeting and drinks with the team. After the small talk and finishing a bottle of French wine, the leader of the Alcatel team complimented me on the information provided to them and wanted me to know that he and his team agreed with my business improvement suggestions. I thanked them and expressed my appreciation for their comments. I wish I could express in words my feelings about what happened next. The leader of the Alcatel group asked me to consider taking over as President of Solid State Systems. Wow! I did not see this coming. They explained their reasoning, and, in their opinion, the executive management had made strategic errors and needed to leave for the business to thrive. They asked me to think about this change and let them know my decision early the following morning. Another sleepless night was in store for me. I could not wait to tell Elaine what had happened that day. She, like me, was so excited and we agreed that I should take their offer.

The next day became the most challenging day of my career. After accepting my new position as President, the Alcatel leadership asked me to plan and implement a strategy that would convert the organization from analog technology to digital technology. As this was one of my notebook suggestions, I was excited to make this change, and I knew exactly how to make it happen. However, the next instruction to me was to bring the company to a profitable position within sixty days. So, I transitioned from an accountant on the verge of being fired to this 140-person manufacturing and sales business leader. Now I thought, "how can I achieve their objectives in such a short time frame? Looking back, I can remember the trauma associated with this transition.

The only way that this could happen was to lay off a significant portion of our employees. The following morning, the French team removed the Solid State executives and called a staff meeting to announce my promotion and what would happen next. Their presentation to our staff was eloquent, concise, and explained the problems with Solid State's operations and strategy, the termination of the executive team, my promotion to President, and the mandate to launch a digital product while still supporting and archiving the old system. After they completed the presentation, it was my turn. First, I complimented our guests on their interest in our company and announced the specifics relating to the change in strategy. Next, I told the employees that we would have to make layoffs; however, I promised to bring as many individuals back to work as the company started to achieve its profitability objectives.

Over the next two days, we processed eighty employee layoffs. I pushed for as much severance time as possible to lessen the blow to our long-term staff members. Alcatel promised to cover these expenses, which would reduce the impact on our operating results. After removing the last employee impacted by the layoff, I called a meeting with the remaining staff to let them know there would be no further layoffs. I explained why their jobs were essential to the organization's new digital strategy. Let the fun begin!

My layoff strategy was to maintain my software engineers and remove most of our hardware engineers. I took the role of engineering project leader, and we began the transformation of our analog ACD switch to a digital platform. I was amazed at the creative transition ideas offered by my software engineers. They were mentally engaged and made daily progress. However, we still were responsible for legacy systems sold previously, and we began receiving several service calls relating to new installations.

My support staff was having problems resolving an overheating issue on one of our circuit boards. They had replaced defective boards in several of our customer locations, but the new circuit boards were also having problems. I started an investigation into this repair issue. I learned the problem started three months prior and that this situation was new to our switch. With this realization, I spoke with our director of manufacturing. He was unaware of any process changes that may have impacted the switch's operations. My next stop was with the purchasing manager. I knew that we subcontracted some of our high-volume circuit boards, and I wanted to determine if this board was one of them. Problem discovered—the purchasing manager had changed subcontractors for this unique board, which coincided with the start of the problem. Upon further investigation, we learned that a critical component on the board was backward, causing the overheating problem. However, at about this time, I started feeling like I was playing the whack-a-mole game as a new problem surfaced each time we corrected a one.

We had a significant client, the Salt River Project, an electric utility that used our switch for customer service and telemarketing. This client was a critical account for us, one that we could use as a high-impact reference. Their call volume was by far the most our switch had processed compared to other clients. Unfortunately, just after we delivered our ACD switch, it would consistently quit working during their highest call volume periods on Tuesday and Thursday evenings. Our remote diagnostics confirmed the switch would completely lose power for an hour during these periods. We generated fake high-volume traffic on our test switch at the office, but we could not duplicate the problem. My engineering staff felt the problem was an over-heating problem causing the system to shut down during peak traffic. Understanding the urgency associated with this problem, we sent two new switches--$125,000 each—one to replace the defective unit and one to have on standby should the problem happen again. Unfortunately, the over-heating continued, so a resolution was necessary, or we risked losing this major client. I decided to send a technician to the site to babysit the switch during these peak periods. What we discovered is funny now, but it was not funny back then. It turns out that the cleaning lady vacuumed the floors on Tuesday and Thursday evenings. Since we were using a standard 110-volt electrical socket, she would unplug our switch and plug her vacuum cleaner. The electrical socket was the only one near where she needed to vacuum. When she finished cleaning, she would plug our system back into the socket, allowing it to reboot. As you can imagine, from that moment on, we hardwired all our electrical connections.

After working with my staff to improve our support function and convert our switches to digital, I began looking into how we might become an international provider. Since we were near the completion of our digital conversion, I learned that we could now mimic the international codes with a few internal software changes that would only take a few months to accomplish. I gave the go-ahead on the additional programming, and we successfully launched a sales effort in South America and Asia. Solid State had an outstanding sales team led by Dave Zovod, an industry veteran, and his team quickly made inroads into the international market by leveraging trade show relationships. As a result, our new switch appeared flexible and rock-solid. I will never forget the picture of our switch on a raft traveling to an island near Bandung, Indonesia.

Mission accomplished! Solid State reached profitability in the sixty-day time frame given to us by Alcatel. Our distributors rallied around our modified switch, and our international sales increased. We went from annual sales of $5 million to a yearly run rate of $14 million. Our growth was exceptional, and I was invited to France to visit Alcatel headquarters to present our turnaround results to the Alcatel team and their superiors. Solid State was beginning to emerge as a strong company in the digital switch marketplace. For the first time, I felt excited to work with synergistic professionals who not only shared my enthusiasm but who also leveraged each other's knowledge, relationships, and experience to broaden the acceptance of our products.

We began making headlines and achieving recognition in the marketplace for our switching capabilities. On November 19, 1990, we announced that the Atlanta Organizing Committee (AOC) would be using our switch for the 1996 Summer Olympic Games to serve as their interface to process the incoming call volume from people around the world seeking information. I had the opportunity to work with Mayor Andrew Young, Billy Payne (President of the AOC), and the AOC staff to plan how to process calls about jobs, licensing, tickets, reservations, and volunteer work. In addition, many of these calls would be in foreign languages. Here is a fun fact: Billy Payne later became the Chairman of the Augusta National Golf Club. We programmed our ACD to meet all the needs of the AOC, and we offered the switch to them at cost. We had correctly anticipated that Atlanta would become the host city for the 1996 Olympics. As soon as the AOC announced their selection, our switch began processing information calls, which grew to more than 6,000 per day. Much to my chagrin, our success with the AOC would be short-lived. Nortel offered the AOC their ACD switch and other telephony products totaling more than $1 million for free, resulting in the AOC asking to return our switch. We agreed to take it back. This setback was a valuable lesson to me about marketing—never underestimate a competitor's aggressiveness to secure a significant account.

Learning from the Nortel mistake, we decided to "invest" our profits as donations of products and services to non-profit organizations to underscore our corporate philanthropy. This action would not only enable us to gain referenceable accounts but would also broaden our ACD applications. On May 21, 1990, we announced a donation of our switch to Boys Town. Boys Town, established in 1917, was a Nebraska children's home providing services and counseling to children in need. Our switch enabled Boys Town to develop a crisis hotline that would operate seven days a week and twenty-four hours a day. I will never forget the uplifting story told by Father Val J. Peter, Executive Director of Boys Town, about the first crisis call received through our system. The call was from a boy in New York City whose father was sexually abusing him. The boy called the crisis hotline number and spoke to a counselor who stayed on the call while notifying the proper authorities. This successful outcome was worth more than short-term profit. We were achieving a new kind of success, and I was excited.

For the first time in my career, I was in a position enabling me to use my vision, creativity, problem-solving, and team-building skills to drive success for our company. I knew I was on the way to building a successful organization that hopefully could be taken public in the future. Ah yes, this was my dream. But, unfortunately, the realization of this dream did not happen.

Shortly after the 60-day turnaround project, Alcatel called to inform me that they wanted to divest Solid State Systems from their organization. Honestly, I was devastated as I recounted all the effort expended toward meeting their mandates. Yes, I had another sleepless night deciding how to process the news. The following day, I decided to take a chance. I called my Alcatel superior and offered to buy the company. To my surprise, he agreed to the purchase and set the price for the company at $6 million; however, I needed to complete the transaction within sixty days. What was it with them and sixty days? I had never raised capital; however, my Controller and I were up for the challenge. We quickly put together a prospectus using the financial notebook I had prepared for Alcatel and updated it for the operating results since their acquisition. We immediately began contacting venture capital and mezzanine financing firms. I was surprised how easy it was to pitch our deal, and we must have presented a compelling opportunity as feedback was positive. One firm, Alliance Capital, was highly interested. The representative, Dr. Bill Gordon, who managed more than $1 billion for the firm, wanted to explore the investment potential further.

Just so you know, I was personally funding the efforts to acquire Solid State, so finding a venture partner became my immediate focus. I convinced Dr. Gordon to take a trip with us through Germany. My goal for the trip was to demonstrate the significant need for lower-cost telephone switching systems in former East Germany and other emerging economies. I purchased two Delta Dream Vacations to save money, which offered a two-for-one special, including flight, car, and hotel. Working with the Delta representative, I arranged to fly four of us to Frankfurt, thinking that it would only take a few hours to drive to Rostock, the place of our first meeting. I never imagined that it would take more than eight hours, but the trip turned out to be one of the most memorable trips of my life.

Each village and small-town had its brewery. Recognizing that our journey would be longer than anticipated, we decided to stop and check out the different beer alternatives in each town. These stops were so much fun, and we could not wait to visit the next village. At our last village stop, we met an attractive barmaid, or "Fräulein," who was topless. We cringed as she brought our brews to the table, holding them tightly to her chest. After leaving this memorable experience, Dr. Gordon took the wheel. With little patience for the traffic, he proceeded to begin passing several cars until a car pulled out of the line of traffic into our lane, forcing us to pull off the highway. The driver got out of his car and approached us, yelling at the top of his lungs. Bill lowered his window and attempted to tell the man we did not speak German and were visitors to the country. Finally, the man quit yelling, returned to his car, and did a little fishtail movement as he pulled back into traffic. I guess this must have signaled everyone not to let us back in line. I still laugh when I think of that trip.

Unfortunately, I was unsuccessful in raising the necessary

capital to buy the company, and I had to turn down the purchase opportunity. Still, I at least had a chance to go through the process. Later, the Alcatel team used their relationships to find a buyer. After the transaction, Alcatel rewarded my efforts with a one-year's salary bonus, which was both unexpected and appreciated.

Lessons Learned

From my bungled attempt to manage a Roberts Furniture Store to achieving international success as President of Solid State Systems/ Alcatel, I perfected several skills. I learned a lot about finance and acquisitions, developed successful sales and engineering teams, closed significant financial transactions, accomplished a business turn-around, expanded my management skills on an international scale, expanded my knowledge and experience with employee relations, and learned how to be a polished executive. My self-awareness and self-confidence developed over time, and fortunately for me, I learned active listening and how to approach situations with an open mind. This process enabled me to become flexible in my approach to social situations. Lastly, I learned to forgive others and myself for not meeting expectations.

CHAPTER 5

Financial and International Leadership

As God's steward, an overseer must be above reproach—not self-absorbed, not quick-tempered, not given to drunkenness, not violent, not greedy for money. 8Instead, he must be hospitable, a lover of good, self-controlled, upright, holy, and disciplined. 9He must hold firmly to the faithful word as it was taught, so that he can encourage others by sound teaching and refute those who contradict it.

—TITUS 1:7–9

As I interviewed with organizations following the sale of Solid State Systems/Alcatel, I became acutely aware of my ability to take the "financial" pulse of a company. I would perform research on each company before the interview, and from this research, I was able to assess where a company's mission did not align with its actions. Thus, I was adept at assessing the big picture and the potential for these companies. Little did I know that my next career opportunity would be sink or swim for my financial expertise.

Federal Home Loan Bank of Georgia, Atlanta, Georgia

I approached a recruiter friend for help in finding my next career move. Although my most recent expertise was telecom-related, he directed me in a new direction. I interviewed to become the accounting manager for the $12 billion Federal Home Loan Bank of Georgia. My interview went well, and I assumed the responsibility of preparing the month-end closing for the bank. Wow—I had never seen a calculator that went into the billions of dollars, nor had I ever had the chance to round numbers to the nearest million-dollar figure. My skills and experience gained from my role at First Railroad and Banking Company came in handy, and it was relatively easy to determine the journal entries needed to complete the month-end close. Three weeks into the job, I closed the month, and the Controller and Assistant Controller let me know their appreciation for my efforts. They were two of the smartest women I have ever met, and each of them had significant banking, regulatory, and accounting knowledge and experience. My work with them was fast-paced and a real challenge. Whenever I had a question, all I had to do was ask, and I would be on my way with the answer.

I began my effort to understand the big picture enabling me to relate my closing duties to the organizational mission. I met the bank's department heads and quickly understood how to consolidate their finances into my closing. I enjoyed interacting with the different department heads and enjoyed listening to their stories about the bank. My only concern was the pay, which was one-third of my previous salary, but I tried to weigh the bank's benefits and the job security to justify the difference. I let my employment search continue while I accepted the challenge of the new job. I made copious notes with charts and outlines to enable me or whoever had the position next to have references for each line item for the financial statements.

Although I mastered the bank's job responsibilities, my continued employment search for a higher-paying position led me to an executive position opening with Conway Data. Once again, I had the choice and the chance to improve my career trajectory. Only later would I realize that my decision to leave the bank would place me outside of the financial industry, thereby closing the door on a future opportunity in banking.

Conway Data, Inc. — Norcross, Georgia

I had the opportunity to interview with Conway Data, Inc. This organization monitored and reported on the world's super projects ($1 billion and above) and assisted companies in real estate planning and acquisition. I met with Mac Conway, a veteran of international development and real estate expansion. He wanted to work with all the mega-builders to find patterns and experiences that would benefit other projects and provide lessons to reduce waste and improve efficiency. He was all about providing a value-add service to his clients. He invited me to become the Executive Director for the World Development Association and the Director of Sales for international clients seeking to introduce real estate leasing opportunities and economic development. I accepted this new challenge with an increase in compensation more than two times the bank salary, plus I received commission on publishing advertisements. Mr. Conway's daughter, Ms. Laura Lyne, became an essential ally to complete challenging assignments. She became a good friend, and her vast expertise and knowledge of real estate and international operations allowed us to accomplish the goals set by Mr. Conway.

As an introduction, Conway is the world's only full-service agency in the global corporate investment industry, with a sixty-five-year-old publications division, a fifty-year-old associate management division, a site selection consulting division, a marketing division, and decades of event management expertise. My new role involved working with Economic Development Agencies worldwide to publish special supplements on their activities to introduce companies to real estate expansion opportunities and best practices in real estate. In addition, my role included planning and implementing international events to foster knowledge-sharing and networking opportunities. For example, I led a team that planned and executed the company's first international super-projects conference in Singapore. The well-attended meeting included the leadership of Bechtel, Fluor Daniel, and several other billion-dollar infrastructure builders. In addition, our programming included networking events to allow conference attendees to share the knowledge and experience with super projects.

I was responsible for our Amsterdam and Singapore offices. The mission for these locations was to work with economic development agencies to promote office locations in Asia and Europe. Our Site World magazine provided insight to companies considering the expansion into new international markets. Our magazine became an essential tool to these companies, and our growth trajectory was positive due to our coverage of real estate within these global markets. My American and foreign nationals staff was highly engaged, talented, and experienced, and they interacted well with our clients.

My memorable experience in the Netherlands was the cultural difference from the United States. Two events happened that opened my eyes to this fact. The first was Queens Day, where anyone could bring their un-needed household goods to the curb for sale. I was in a college town, Utrecht, when this event took place, and it was like a massive yard sale. I enjoyed my experience, which included bands, food, and scores of people having a wonderful time together. My other memorable event happened in my hotel one evening. I had been traveling and working long hours and decided to use the hotel sauna and fitness rooms. I had been in the sauna for about five minutes when five attractive and naked female flight attendants entered the sauna with me. My cultural education expanded when I realized that clothes were optional in this sauna. Having just finished exercising, I was still wearing my workout shorts and did not know what to do next. Finally, after frantically trying to decide my next move, I decided to say hello and asked them if they were enjoying their hotel stay. They then informed me that they worked for KLM, the Dutch Airline, and this hotel was a routine layover for them. Although this experience was awkward for me, they were at ease and talkative. After a short while, I told them I had to go and hoped to see them again.

Although I was enjoying my job, two life-changing events happened, inspiring me to explore new opportunities. First, my dad passed away in October 1992 after a major heart attack. His sudden death was a shock to me as we never had the opportunity to rebuild a close relationship due to my time away; however, he had become that perfect grandad to my children and my brother's children. I am glad they had the opportunity to develop and enjoy a positive relationship with him; however, his passing was a wake-up call to use my remaining time on earth in impactful ways that would be exciting to me.

I recognized that my success in my position at Conway Data could lead to increased responsibilities. As I expected, when I returned from my father's funeral, they asked me to consider taking on new marketing responsibilities. Although these new responsibilities could have been a new challenge, I honestly did not find this to be an exciting option. Fortunately for me, the next day, I received a call from Dr. Bill Gordon, my friend from Solid State Systems. He alerted me to a start-up company seeking to become the second telecom carrier in Russia. He had introduced me to them as a candidate for their Chief Operating Officer. Naturally, this opportunity was attractive. It would allow me to use my telecommunications expertise and gain hands-on experience implementing a new strategic venture in a foreign country.

A. O. Rustel/IBCS — Moscow, Russia

I accepted the position with IBCS and became responsible for leading startup operations in Moscow and other cities for satellite communications. The headquarters for the company was near Boston, but my primary location was in Moscow. The two founders, Arnold Freedman and Jim Hickman, were schooled on the Russian political scene and had been entrepreneurs in other Russian ventures. They were true visionaries who were trying to capitalize on the fall of the Soviet Union—the reader may want to review the August 1991 Soviet coup d'état attempt. Their strategy was sound, but we were attempting to sell systems into the Russian Republic, which, looking back, was a mistake. Instead, we should have been quickly placing systems in the major cities throughout Russia and creating new telephone companies. I believe now that this strategy would have attracted significant capital funding to further the buildout.

I would work in Russia for five to seven-week periods and then come back home for one to two weeks. Russia's existing telecom infrastructure was antiquated and unreliable, which provided a unique opportunity for us to install an alternative infrastructure. My goal was to establish satellite-based communications that would serve as an overlay network to transmit and receive business communication from Western companies seeking to do business in Russia.

The two founders formed an American/Russian joint-venture—A. O. Rustel—and developed a relationship with Deutsche Telecom to become our downlink connection to the global telecommunications network. They also had hired Gyorgi Kolmogorov to work with the American partners to navigate the Russian political environment.

Kolmogorov, the name we called him, was the former Deputy Telecommunications Minister for Russia. His people network, coupled with this knowledge and experience, helped me determine the strategic areas to offer satellite communications. He was a fun-loving individual, and I am sure it must have been hard for him to go from being driven around in limousines with flags on the front to working in a start-up company. A Russian translator, also named Gyorgi, went with me to all business meetings and translated my conversations in the office. At first, it was difficult to talk through a translator, but later I learned key Russian words that enabled me to follow conversations in real-time. The three of us traveled throughout Russia meeting people Kolmogorov knew through his former executive capacity. The trains were modern and always arrived on time. Many trips were during the winter, and I felt as if someone had transported me into the Dr. Zhivago movie. The countryside was beautiful, and all the people were friendly.

I also made several trips to Bonn, Germany, the headquarters for Deutsche Telecom, to work on implementation details for our satellite downlinks. I negotiated the purchase of bandwidth on the KU-band of Intelsat 6, 60 degrees east, which enabled us to use smaller satellite dishes and offer higher quality communications. I found a picture of me signing this deal with Deutsche Telecom executives, and it brought back all the memories of my efforts to close this deal. After completing this transaction, A. O. Rustel was able to offer communications services.

I traveled to many former Russian Republics—Krasnoyarsk, Kyrgyzstan, Uzbekistan, Tyumen, Novosibirsk, and Irkutsk—and several smaller locations. Each trip was educational and a new adventure. One of my first business trips with Kolmogorov in Siberia (sorry, I do not remember the place) was to a "secret" city (Krasnoyarsk 26) that, according to our host, was unknown to the United States. I remember the conversation well; the man in charge bragged about being a loyal communist, and in his opinion, western capitalism was enigmatic. I strictly followed a conviction to never discuss political issues in a country where I was a guest, so I acknowledged his opinion and attempted to move the conversation quickly back to telecommunications. We did not consummate a deal, but it was a memorable experience.

Another unusual experience happened as I was visiting Perm, Russia, to close a deal with an entrepreneur who wanted to compete with the existing network. Upon arriving, I was arrested and taken to the "Politsiya," a Russian police station. The police were yelling at Gyogi, my translator, saying that my credentials were inadequate because I did not have a trip visa. Russia had previously instituted a Republic-wide visa removing the requirement to have individual travel visas; however, Perm did not approve this change. After two hours of this nonsense, I put a $100 bill in my passport and told Gyogi to ask the officer to again look at my credentials. Within five minutes, he approved my visa, and we were on our way. Funny how that happened.

My next cultural learning experience happened at a closing. My translator and I were trying to obtain signed documents. I had a portable computer and printer that I used to complete forms and to print them for signing. In the middle of printing the signing documents, my computer battery ran out of juice. The client told me this was not a problem and instructed his secretary to bring in a power supply to complete the transaction. While waiting on the device, our client pulled out a bottle of vodka. Russia was known for its drinking, but I did not realize that it would be a part of consummating a transaction. Gyorgi explained that we must drink the entire bottle out of respect for our host and to celebrate the completed transaction. By the time the power supply arrived, I was feeling the effects of the alcohol. When I saw the power supply, I started laughing so hard tears started streaming down my face. The power unit was six feet by two feet in size. Their engineers had developed the power supply to mimic our 120-volt 60-cycle American power requirements. Much to my chagrin, I lost the picture of my computer plugged into this massive device. Nevertheless, the power supply worked perfectly, and I was able to complete and print the contract.

From that day forward, I took five people to every deal closing for cultural reasons, and I took along an extra battery pack. There were several other cultural differences I noted. For example, wedding rings on the right hand; handshakes in a doorway indicated a fleeting relationship; odd numbers of flowers for get-togethers since even numbers were for funerals, and one should always have a toast ready for each dining occasion.

After closing a few deals and ramping up business development, we hired several Russian engineers and office staff who worked closely with our American team. The office was bustling with activity, and each day was long and tiresome. One day, my secretary informed me several men were waiting to see me. This impromptu meeting was unexpected as I had just returned from a trip and had no appointments scheduled. She escorted the men into my office, and we took seats around my meeting table. The men were wearing black leather coats and were obviously in good physical shape. Once seated, my secretary provided coffee and cookies to our group. Then one of the men told me that he was concerned about my security and the security of our office. My guests then pulled out pistols and placed them on the table. The man said they had walked right through the guard structure at our building entrance, and he wanted me to hire his company to protect our staff. As calm as I could be, I asked him to give me the particulars relating to how we might work together. After getting his pricing and other information about the transaction, I thanked them for bringing this need to my attention and asked if they could give me a day to talk to my Russian partner, which they approved. After they left, I called Elaine, my wife, to tell her about my day. She was not too thrilled to learn that I was mob shopping.

My Russian partner told me to do the deal. He said there were 1,500 organized mobs (security firms) in Russia. I accepted the proposed arrangement and received a door guard for twelve hours each day, travel security when needed, and frequent security checks on our premises. The enhanced security could not have come at a more opportune time.

In October 1993, the Russian Parliament and President Yeltzin were at a standoff. The Russian Parliament controlled the White House and declared president Yeltzin's decree to abolish the legislature null and void. The parliament voted to impeach Yeltzin and elected an interim president, Mr. Aleksandr Rutskoy. The standoff became bloody, with many people killed or wounded. The military tanks began firing at the White House to scare Parliament into retreat. I was advised not to leave my apartment as it was not safe to be outside. A few days after the coup took place, I visited the hotel across from the White House, where I witnessed rooms with bullet holes and broken windows. This event was another scary incident that I got to observe. This experience is still fresh on my mind as I write this chapter.

Lessons Learned

In early 1995, I chose to leave Russia and the employment of IBCS, as the political environment was not healthy. I had made some wonderful friends during my time in Russia, and the experiences were both memorable and life-changing. However, my gut told me it was time to leave. A year later, my good friend, Paul Tatum, was gunned down as he stepped from the subway in Moscow. He and I had tried to change the way business was done in Russia, and I was so sorry to see his efforts come to such a tragic end (US entrepreneur killed in Moscow).

I learned something about myself in the positions mentioned in this chapter. I am not a person that likes repetitive and routine functions. I am a creative and curious individual who seeks to be involved in developing and implementing strategic visions. These positions enabled me to become more confident in my abilities and made me acutely aware of the positive changes that technology would have in the future. My experiences with A. O. Rustel introduced me to the potential of broadband, and this knowledge would lead the way to my next career adventure.

CHAPTER 6

Becoming a Technology Entrepreneur

Consider it pure joy, my brothers and sisters, whenever
you face trials of many kinds because you know that
the testing of your faith produces perseverance.

—JAMES 1:2–3

In August 1995, the vision for how technology would drive productivity became as clear to me as the nose on my face. The United States would need a broadband infrastructure for the future of communications and network development. With the knowledge and experience gained from my work in Russia, I was ready to pursue becoming one of the first, if not the first, broadband service provider in the United States. Elaine, my wife, and I learned we were on the front-end of this strategy as no one else seemed to be focusing on this opportunity due to the many regulatory barriers in place at the time. In addition, business customers had not yet embraced the power of the Internet. Almost everyone still had single services with the telephone, ISP, and CATV companies, so I knew the offering of bundled services to these customers could be a winning strategy. As I attended business meetings put on by Bear Stearns and Lehman Brothers, I quickly realized most businesses were considering the addition of a website. However, very few HTML programmers were available, and the demand for website services was growing. With companies adding interactive websites, I could readily see that broadband service providers would be critical for real-time access. Prodigy and AOL offered content; however, accessing their content over dial-up was slow and required significant patience.

Further research led us to learn about the Telecommunications Act of 1996, which could open up the communications market to competition and allow power and gas utilities to use their city network infrastructure and customer relationships to become a value-add partner to communications companies. This research informed us that utilities and municipalities could potentially provide capital in addition to their customer relationships and power-line network. While searching online, we found a strategic plan for a city in California that wanted to overlay its telephone network with broadband infrastructure. This information, coupled with our other research findings, enabled us to conclude how to move forward. Elaine and I spent weeks developing our business plan and how to present it to investors. Now, all we needed was a name for our company.

UtiliCom Networks, LLC (UCN)

Elaine came home from jogging and blurted out the perfect name for our new company, UtiliCom Networks. This name succinctly described our business plan, which was to partner with electric and gas utilities to bring the power of broadband communications and the pricing advantage of bundled services to their customers. We would become the preferred provider of communications services by partnering with electric and gas utilities and use the power-line network to connect business and residential customers. At least we now had a plan I could use to begin the business development and capital procurement process.

Using the $20,000 severance received from IBCS, I hired two engineers to assist me in presentations and network design. After perfecting our broadband network strategy, we began to call on utilities in Massachusetts to introduce our approach. Almost immediately, we received a contract from Taunton's Municipal Utility to design a broadband network that would allow them to become an internet service provider (ISP). The $50,000 for this project enabled us to expand our search for capital and partners and provided us a good reference. This money-raising process was new and complex, as I had previously never raised any money to support my ideas. Even though I contacted many venture firms, we were unsuccessful in acquiring any capital funding before running through my severance and customer funding.

Nevertheless, Elaine and I firmly believed that this opportunity was worth pursuing, even if the downside risk would put us into bankruptcy. Little did we know that we would use all the cash advances from our charge cards and face foreclosure of our home after missing five monthly payments before we would receive an outside capital infusion. However, one significant opportunity did present itself at this time.

Prodigy was an internet service that had access to important content and to telephone company distribution networks. One of my company's advisers told me that the owners of Prodigy were looking to sell the company. My thought process was that an acquisition like this would enable us to become the premier provider of DSL (digital-subscriber-line) connectivity, gain access to content and applications, and pick up a large customer base. We were able to meet with the company representative about the transaction, and over the next few weeks, we reached an agreement on the deal. We would purchase Prodigy and all its assets for an upfront payment. Part of the deal was that Telmex would offer us the same amount contract to continue to provide content and services to its customers. With an agreement in hand, we went to the Bank of Mitsubishi to fund the deal based on the collateral of Prodigy and the Telmex contract. Unfortunately, in the end, the bank could not get approval to lend us the upfront payment, and we lost the opportunity; however, for a few days, we had the chance of a lifetime. Now it was time to get back to network planning and equipment selection.

It was easy to find engineers with telephone, CATV, and Internet experience to design the broadband network. We chose a Nortel telecommunications switch, storage arrays from EMC Corporation, and selected network routers and other products from Racal Datacom. We determined that Scientific Atlanta could provide the balance of the network equipment. The huge gaping hole was systems integration. We needed a billing system that would take customer data from disparate services and consolidate them on an invoice while at the same time figuring federal and state fees. This system did not exist on the open market and had to be custom developed. Fortunately for UCN, we hired Mark Rein, a technology and system integration expert. In just a few months, he did the impossible. Our billing system was a one-of-a-kind system that functioned perfectly, and it defied all odds against us. We watched as other companies struggled in this area. The only question I ask myself today is, "why didn't we patent our billing system design?" I firmly believe that UCN was ultimately able to become an integrated service provider due to Mark's expertise. After UCN and other technology ventures, Mark is now a senior executive with the U.S. International Development Finance Corporation.

Scientific Atlanta was a leader in the broadband industry and a recognized provider of equipment to the CATV industry. I made a business call to get a quote on some of the critical components of our network. During my visit, I met a Vice President {name withheld} that took an immediate interest in our venture. As we talked, I could tell he knew the CATV industry exceptionally well. He immediately suggested utility customers who would be interested in our broadband strategy. After further discussions, he decided to leave Scientific Atlanta and join our company, and I am so glad he did. We worked well together, and he added further credibility to my management team as our VP of Sales.

With only $1,700 left in my bank account and no further access to any funding, Elaine and I made the difficult decision to spend those funds on one more attempt to find an investor. My VP of Sales and I took a trip to Williams Companies in Tulsa, OK. Williams was a natural gas provider to gas utilities and used its infrastructure to offer fiber connectivity to areas within its network. Our presentation was well-received, and Williams became the investment partner that we needed to implement our strategy.

UCN next closed a partnership arrangement with Southern Indiana Gas and Electric Company (SIGECO) to form a broadband service provider to customers in the utility's network area. The venture became known as Sigecom. The chairman of SIGECO and I spent a lot of time getting to know each other during the 1996 Olympics in Atlanta. We formed a good relationship, which ultimately led to the formation of the partnership. This venture became our singular focus, and I hired Rich Wadman, a CATV industry executive, to run the business venture. He did a great job building a team and working with my staff to implement the operations. With my dream now realized, I would soon learn that certain board members would try to oust me from the company—more on this later. My start-up company was not only doing well, but it had also reached $25 million in revenue in just four years. I later introduced Blackstone Capital to the company, and they elected to purchase an 80 percent interest in the company for a $100 million investment into UCN in early 2000 (Blackstone, 2000).

I learned so much about myself and how to do business in this venture. I had the unrelenting drive to make this opportunity successful. Unfortunately, my fear of financial failure kept me from having any balance in my life. I remember one Christmas holiday season when I was the only one working at the end of the year. I wanted to find the funding to pay for UCN's operations and to pay for the buildout of our Sigecom partnership, and I was not going to give up trying. It was late on the last day of the year when I put a call into ATT Capital. Because most people were on holiday, an executive answered the phone. I quickly introduced my company and told him why I was calling. This call was the catalyst that led to UCN receiving a $45 million line of credit for the broadband buildout and operating capital. This future cash infusion was great, but I was unprepared for the political games ahead.

I learned the hard way the importance of never losing control of your Board of Directors and always question venture capital providers' motives. As mentioned earlier, trusting others has always been difficult for me, and I should not have let my guard down at UCN. We hired a venture firm out of Boston to assist us in raising capital. The firm {name withheld} would receive a percentage of any investment funds and an advisory fee. Before negotiating the ATT Capital facility I had arranged, the venture firm came to me with an amendment to our agreement, adding a clause allowing them to receive a percentage for "all" funding achieved while under their agreement, no matter who brought in the funding. This change enabled them to receive $1 million when the ATT deal closed, which they had not earned. I also learned that the Board of Directors could override the percentage stock control you have within the organization. Even though I was the founder and majority owner, the venture firm convinced the Board that we needed a CEO with more in-depth experience running a large company and better name recognition. I will never forget board members asking me to leave the company I started. The funny thing is that even with their new high-power CEO, the firm was unsuccessful in raising capital. I wish I could have seen their facial expressions when I was the one who brought Blackstone Capital to the negotiating table and when they learned that I had taken an executive position with Callahan Associates International. UCN continued to grow after the Blackstone investment. They were able to divest their investment in 2006, selling it to WOW for approximately $117 million as part of a transaction liquidating UtiliCom Networks and its assets (Evansville Courier & Press, 2006). At the time of the sale, the Sigecom network served more than 75,000 customers and 5,500 businesses.

As I reflect on this experience, I remember the role Alicia, my daughter, and Elaine played in the success of UCN. Alicia served as our "everything that needed doing in the office" person, and her attention to detail was outstanding. She prepared our brochures and meeting folders, as well as helping Elaine with office administration. The two of them worked long hours and under stressful situations. I do believe that UCN would not have been successful without their support and dedication to our mission. I can only imagine how much the hiring of the venture firm cost Elaine and me; however, other than the money potentially lost, we did accomplish our dream of building a successful enterprise. I was fortunate to find and hire several true professionals that partnered with me on this opportunity.

Callahan Associates International

After finalizing my severance package with UCN and obtaining my deferred compensation, I called my friend, Bill Gordon, to advise what I should do next. Bill was now a founder of Callahan Associates

International (CAI), and he invited me to meet with Dick Callahan (the other founder) and the other CAI partners. All the meetings went well, and I later met Mr. Callahan, who would have the final say on any employment offer. He was formerly the head of US West International and a pioneer in the broadband industry. We had a phenomenal conversation. My people network was strong, especially with financing sources within Bear Stearns and other venture firms. After talking for approximately an hour, the meeting ended, and I was offered the position of Global Development Partner with the responsibility to find acquisition companies and content providers that would enhance CAI's European broadband network.

I quickly learned that I was in an actual executive position. I prepared for a trip with my new boss, a CAI partner, to an overseas meeting and reserved my seat in coach. As I arrived at the airport, the partner stated that we needed to have a working flight, and he upgraded my flight to first class. I received instructions that we should always fly first class and stay in upscale lodging to enhance my chances of meeting synergistic people and to enable my business guests to meet in a comfortable atmosphere. This mandate was a departure from any of my prior experiences, but I soon learned the value of this approach when I experienced successful meetings with executives of target companies. The CAI partners and I worked tirelessly to achieve the objectives of CAI. I appreciated that my boss was an excellent mentor to me and valued his Christian fellowship.

I traveled extensively for CAI to meet with acquisition prospects in Asia and Europe. The job was like traveling at the speed of light. We were laser-focused on building value for the CATV networks. At one point, I had nineteen target companies ready to move to the next stage. This potential was great but terrible at the same time. Unfortunately, while in Japan, I learned CAI was not prepared to fund any of the transactions. I remember the conversation with Mr. Callahan where I briefed him on the potential acquisition transactions and expressed my frustration due to not being able to close any of them. He was a polished executive who listened intently and helped me through my frustration while at the same time advising me on how to work with my prospects. I always enjoyed talking with him and watching him in meetings. I learned so much from working with him. Watching him in a discussion was like watching a fisherman throw a baited line in the water, seeing him wait on a nibble, and then snatching the line tight when he knew he had the fish hooked.

I was able to bring Mark Rein (formerly with UtiliCom Networks) into the CAI venture to help set up the iCloud data centers and help CAI with CATV integration in Spain and other areas. Patrice Gorin became business development manager and impromptu French teacher. He was from France and had graduated at the top of his class. Three other vital hires on my team were Tacis Gavoyannis and Paolo Capuani for business development and operations and Felipe Zarate for finance. Felipe's ability to create accurate financial projections and model target prospects was a confidence booster.

I mentioned Prodigy as the UCN deal that slipped through my fingers, but who would have expected this to happen twice. My boss and I negotiated an agreement to acquire 80 percent of XStream for $5 million. The company was needing cash to expand and had hired HBC to represent them. The HBC representative knew CAI as a reputable company and therefore accepted an exclusive letter of intent to perform due diligence on the company. After spending some time with XStream's financials, meeting the team, and other due diligence, we concluded XStream could be a primary content provider to the CAI European CATV network and provide additional revenue to our organization from Internet services. We next approached our financing sources to fund the transaction; however, our funding sources had just financed the purchase of a CATV network and declined to finance further initiatives until they had seen some operating results from this investment. We worked long hours and tirelessly to complete this transaction, but we could not raise the capital, and ultimately we withdrew from the letter of intent. A short time later, we read that France's Liberty Surf acquired XStream for $68 million (Internet News, 2000). I bet our finance sources regretted that they did not finance the transaction.

As part of my CAI role, I became a founding CEO for two broadband companies, Nupremis and CAI Broadband Wireless. After successfully raising $25 million for these ventures (Denverpost, 2000), I used a portion of the proceeds along with a cash and equipment infusion from Compaq to create one of the first iCloud application providers. Our data centers were in London, New York, and Colorado, with a testing facility in Hungary. To add critical engineering and technology support, I led the acquisitions of Centera Information Systems, InterWare, and NewEraCom. In addition, we raised $55 million to fund the purchase of broadband wireless licenses enabling the CAI Broadband expansion into Switzerland.

The Bass Brothers calculated the value of the two companies at over $1 billion. I beamed when I thought of one day realizing the value of my 1.5% ownership. However, I remember hearing the phrase "never to count your chickens before they hatch." This statement became relevant when the internet bubble burst in 2000. Everything that we had been pursuing collapsed. Customers backed out of contract negotiations, financing sources withdrew their support, and internal relationships started to show the stress. On a status update phone call with the new President and COO of CAI's European Cable Operations, I got into a heated argument over what to do next with Nupremis and ended up resigning on the spot. Although this choice cost me a year's salary as severance, I was glad to leave amidst all the uncertainty about the future.

I was renting a farmhouse just outside of Boulder, CO, and I did not want to give it up, but after that call, I shipped my personal belongings back home, sold my car, and booked a flight back to Boston.

Lessons Learned

Certain events in this chapter represent the most emotional times in my life. I learned that there would be situations in life that will challenge you in ways you may never expect. This chapter was a reminder of the significance of developing self-awareness, self-knowledge, self-efficacy, and self-regulation. You may also need to establish boundaries or guardrails to avoid reacting to negative emotions surrounding events. I learned that I could not control events and people; however, I could manage my response to situations.

Broadband technology will significantly impact our lives into the future, so start getting used to change. I wrote the next chapter to give you some insight into my vision for technology. As you will readily recognize, there are many facets of technology that we will be using in the years to come.

CHAPTER 7

My Vision for the Future of Technology

If anyone builds on this foundation using gold, silver, costly stones, wood, hay or straw, their work will be shown for what it is, because the day will bring it to light. It will be revealed with fire, and the fire will test the quality of each person's work. If what has been built survives, the builder will receive a reward. If it is burned up, the builder will suffer loss but yet will be saved—even though only as one escaping through the flames.

—1 Corinthians 3:12–15

What is technology? Most people see technology as devices such as smartphones, computers, or voice-activated items. Try asking someone to define technology. You will receive various answers, usually based on the person's experiences with electronic access equipment, such as computers, automobiles, planes, and smartphones. Wright, Grubbs, and Strimel (2019) defined technology as follows: "Technology is the application of knowledge, tools, and skills to solve problems and extend human capabilities. Technology is any modification of the natural world done to fulfill human needs and desires." Knowing this, you can now recognize that hammers, screwdrivers, pencils, erasures, shoes, and clothes are technology.

Technology is constantly changing to meet the needs of users. I was recently traveling by plane to Columbia, South Carolina. Sitting next to me was a child who could not have been more than three years of age. His mother had given him a magazine to explore. I had to laugh when I saw the child try and swipe the pages to get to a new page. This young person had learned that you swipe the screen of a laptop or eBook to change the page. How many of us have a Kindle or other device that we use to read books, documents, spreadsheets, magazines, or emails? Our lives have benefitted from technologists who used their skills, knowledge, and tools to make visual media accessible on various electronic devices.

If I were defining technology, I would add curiosity, creativity, and perseverance to the definition. How can you solve a problem if you do not even see the problem? Have you ever watched Shark Tank? Each episode highlights entrepreneurs whose curiosity, determination, and problem-solving ability have improved or created some artifact or service that enhances our capabilities. Today, thanks to individuals seeking to solve problems, technology such as drones, cryptocurrency, sharing software (Uber, Lyft, Airbnb), 3-D printers, nanotechnology, machine to machine/human connectivity (Internet of Things), medical imaging and devices, wireless, broadband, space travel, and so much more have expanded our productivity. Like Eli Whitney's cotton gin, technology has allowed us to mass produce items; thereby, revolutionizing the speed of order fulfillment and creating inventory supply/demand success. You can readily see these improvements when you think about the manufacturing and delivery logistics that have enabled Amazon, Walmart, and other distributors to improve delivery times significantly. So, you may be wondering, since I have worked in technology my entire career, what do I anticipate for future technological advancements that will impact our lives?

First, quantum computing and quantum mechanics will revolutionize the speed of data transfer and system operations. Suffice it to say that working to structure subatomic particles and using light to store and deliver data is above my understanding. Still, I recognize that quantum engineering applied in nanotechnology will enable us to make things smaller and faster. I expect to see this technology enable new applications that improve computing power and assist human-to-machine and machine-to-machine applications in monitoring and controlling all types of appliances (wearables, medical, and communications).

SpaceX and Blue Horizon working with NASA will enable space travel to become another commercial platform for delivering goods and services, shorten supply chains and delivery times, and allow opportunities for human travel. In addition, NASA will advance the potential for deep space exploration through robotics, communications, and construction technologies. Space exploration will also become another venue for mining minerals and discovery.

We will see advancements in autonomous and flying vehicles to include farm equipment, drones, personal vehicles, offering new opportunities for shared services and enabling lower-cost ownership, and eliminating inefficiency due to downtime. In addition, robotics will continue to advance in human-like capabilities and replace or augment services such as security guards, sales activities, guides, home/yard management, childcare, product demonstrations, and so much more.

I envision the Internet of Things will continue to connect devices, people, and networks in new and exciting ways. For this to happen, advancements in artificial intelligence applications will continue to mature. Artificial intelligence (AI) will become advanced intelligence and move beyond quickly sorting information and begin using patterns and data mining to make informed decisions. For example, if someone has a wearable with IoT technology embedded, it could detect a heart or respiratory malfunction and immediately call both the user and emergency centers.

Further advancements in data networking and blockchain applications enabled by 5G, WIFI 6, and miniaturizations of networking components will allow the latency to become irrelevant as data transfer speeds begin to mimic real-time. This increase in speed will enable significant advancements in cyber-security and in virtual and augmented reality applications. We will be able to participate in group settings virtually as if we were in a different location. The way we interact with our environment will significantly change. Tele-Health augmented by robotics and medical imaging in real-time will create alternatives for selected surgeries and health management. Shankland and Ryan (2020) penned an article on CNET about Neuralink, a new device invented by Elon Musk that is attempting to connect computer-to-brain applications for advance neural treatments and learning.

Another anticipated change will be the reliance on iCloud services for data storage and retrieval, which, coupled with blockchain, will forever change financial transactions and banking. This change will create the need for different miniaturized access devices, each benefitting from real-time access to stored data in the Cloud. In addition, data security will be enhanced by blockchain applications and edge security, offering less baggage on the network.

I believe we will see a transition to alternative energy and batteries. Solar power cells currently operate at about 33 percent efficiency. Nanotechnology and new chemical structures will enable efficiency increases to above 60 percent. At around this same time, I expect battery storage capacity to exceed its current capacity. Battery power is quickly surpassing fuel combustion engines as a preferred provider of energy. Consider Chip Yates' entrepreneurial advancements in using electric systems to power vehicles (<u>Yates Electrospace Corporation, n.d.</u>). The company is known for designing, building, and flying the world's fastest electric aircraft and developing and constructing megawatt-class electric propulsion systems. His disruptive technologies have earned him wide recognition in the field of electric propulsion. I would expect that within the next ten years, we will see our dependence on oil and gas as energy sources significantly decrease in favor of alternative energy sources and battery advancements.

Of course, there will continue to be improvements in smart technologies: home/business automation, smart city infrastructures, healthcare monitoring, cell phones, surveillance, communications, manufacturing, energy, networking, chemical engineering, and application access. I believe the technology of the future (five to twenty years) will change the way we live, work, and communicate. Technology innovations will be constant, and even though these changes will be exciting, they will also be challenging at the same time. We will see many new applications and processes. My only advice is to buckle up and enjoy the ride.

There will also be many opportunities to invest in these technologies. Maybe you will be like Jeff Bezos, who made a small investment in Google in 1998 and earned billions of dollars in profit (<u>Business Insider, 2018</u>). Hopefully, this discussion of the future will open your mind to an investment opportunity enabling you to become our next billionaire. I currently have investments in companies that are developing the technologies mentioned in this short discussion. If you also make investment decisions to buy shares of companies working in future technologies, try to hold these investments for a minimum of five years to enable their products and services to mature and become value adds for businesses and consumers.

Investing in emerging technologies is not for the faint of heart. Frankly, the process of deciding on an investment strategy is not simple. It would help if you examined your risk tolerance, developed a financial plan, decided on income versus long-term appreciation, and determined whether to diversify. Even though I was a Certified Financial Planner, I turned to an investment advisor to help me sort out these various decisions. For more than twenty years, I have worked with Mr. Brian McNeil, a Vice President with Merrill Lynch. Over the years, I recognized that risking money can be emotional. Brian has always taken the emotions out of any advice to me, which has had positive results.

One time I called him about a stock that was declining in value and was down twenty-five percent. I was frantic and concerned about losing money. He then said something that I will never forget, "Equities may move in either direction. This move may have nothing to do with the fundamentals of the investment, so focus on the long-term objectives and do not let any market or specific investment fluctuation derail your financial plan." He was correct, the stock more than recovered over time, and I am thankful for having a professional assist me in managing my investment portfolio.

Lessons Learned

The potential for growth in technology applications is mind-boggling. My advice is to look for applications that will benefit you both in life and as an investor. Artificial intelligence will optimize virtual intrusions (advertisements, data mining) into our use of technology, so we must try and use the discernment I spoke about earlier to help us separate the "wheat from the chaff."

Technology can have both positive and negative aspects. I purposely avoided in my above discussion any predictions about the unethical uses of technology. However, ethics should come into play when unscrupulous inventors explore dark areas that destroy property or injure people. Examples include cloning, surveillance drones, and artificial intelligence designed to invade privacy or exploit terrorism. For example, genetic engineering (gain-of-function) is most likely the cause behind the Covid-19 pandemic. Therefore, we should voice concerns when we see technology used in ways that may be harmful and detrimental to social norms and our way of life.

Technology is changing at a breakneck pace now, and for many people, this speed can be intimidating. For example, just in the past few weeks, non-fungible tokens (NFTs). NFTs are unique assets that exist online and use a digital ledger to record ownership. A similar digital revolution occurs with cryptocurrency, where these digital files trade outside the typical banking infrastructure. The attempt to keep up with these changes in technology may be frustrating and stressful.

My suggestion is to focus on and use the technologies you feel comfortable using and allow newer technologies to become mainstream, i.e., tested and accepted. Lastly, if you invest in emerging technology companies and do not have the time to perform market research, consider engaging an investment advisor to help guide you.

CHAPTER 8

Becoming an Educator

Whatever you find to do with your hands, do it with
all your might, for in Sheol, where you are going, there
is no work or planning or knowledge or wisdom.

—ECCLESIASTES 9:10

*T*raveling home after I resigned from Callahan Associates International, an unexpected blessing happened. I was sitting in my first-class seat with no one next to me. Shortly after takeoff, the flight attendant told me she was bumping a passenger seated in coach to the aisle seat next to me. A few minutes later, a man took the empty seat and introduced himself. "Hi, I am Dr. Jud Carlberg, and I am flying home for my wife's birthday," he said. I will never forget those words because he told this story of our first encounter many times in the future. We both ordered a glass of wine as the flight attendant asked us for our drink and our meal choices. When she brought the wine, I offered a toast to Jan, his wife, and wished for them to have a wonderful birthday celebration. He then told me he was the president of Gordon College, a Christian liberal arts college in Wenham, Massachusetts, and noted he had been in his position for twenty years. I let him know about what had just happened to me, and he offered some comforting remarks while pulling a booklet from his briefcase.

The booklet appeared to be a strategic plan (I saw the cover of the manuscript). As Jud began reading and opening some fold-out pages, I recognized that this was a communications network design. I told him I could not help but notice the design and asked him if it was a design for broadband services. Our conversation from there was so focused that time just flew by. As we began eating our dinners, he praised my broadband knowledge and asked me to visit him at the college in a couple of weeks to continue our discussion. We then made small talk while we were readying for landing in Boston. I always smile when I see a God-wink in my life, and I know that this was one of those.

Gordon College

ERC—the initials of my wife's name—was formed as a consulting company. Enterprise Resource and Capital (the full name) would seek short- or long-term consulting opportunities to offer services of interim executive leadership (CEO, CFO, COO, CIO), and this formation was timely. Armed with my new business cards and company brochure outlining my experience, I made an appointment for a follow-up visit with Dr. Carlberg. Gordon College had a beautiful campus, and it was fun seeing the students studying in the grass areas and talking with each other. I stopped and spoke to a group of students to get directions to Dr. Carlberg's office. One student must have felt empowered as he volunteered to take me there. I guess it was a big deal to meet with the college president, and the student asked why I was visiting. He quickly wanted to know if I was a new professor, which, when I told him no, he seemed somewhat disappointed. Anyway, I soon made it to Dr. Carlberg's office. His office was in a beautiful stone building called Frost Hall named after Ms. Martha Dodge Frost, whose donation enabled the college to move to the North Shore of Massachusetts. The dedication of Frost Hall was in April 1917. By the way, there is a book written by Belmonte (2017) entitled A. J. Gordon: An Epic Journey of Faith and Pioneering Vision is an excellent read about the history of Gordon College. From the college's website (Gordon College), here is a brief description:

> Gordon College is a distinctive blend: an outstanding nationally ranked liberal arts institution that retains its roots in the Christian faith, a strong residential community, and a splendid location—just north of the intellectual hub of Boston and right near the shoreline of Cape Ann. Our faith is the foundation for all that we are—individually, collectively, and institutionally. With a spirit of support and collaboration, we are set free in Christ to think critically, engage new ideas, and pursue truth.

Dr. Carlberg—Jud, as he asked me to call him—was ready for our meeting and had invited his senior and technological staff to join our discussion. Jud told the group how we met and asked me to expand our design discussions from our earlier plane trip conversation. Elaine and I had done significant research on the college, comparing its digital offering to other liberal arts colleges. Armed with this research, I explained the importance of offering students access to their work off-campus and having the proper amount of downstream bandwidth to allow audio/video streaming and access to websites and documents. In addition, I mentioned the importance of offering instructional design assistance and storage for after-class access to instructor presentations. After about two hours, Jud excused the group and took me to lunch at the college cafeteria.

I enjoyed interacting with everyone, and I felt they also appreciated my suggested improvements to their network design.

At lunch, Jud asked me questions covering endowment investments, staff issues, building plans, and several other planning-related issues. I did my best to give him my knowledge and experience related to each item of concern. After completing lunch, he turned to me and asked me to become the college's CIO and a member of the President's Cabinet. It took me no time to say yes, and I looked forward to starting work with ERC's first client.

I then met June Bodoni, Russ Leathe, and Dave Sweet, the key personnel working with technology. Honestly, I was awestruck by their dedication to the college. Listening to their stories and learning about the history of Gordon College was not only inspiring, but it was also motivational. June was the senior staff person, Dave was the senior technologist who seemed to be the point person for video and audio equipment, and Russ was the technology operations expert. I loved working with these people and their staff, and they accepted me immediately, which was a blessing I had not expected.

Dr. Carlberg had given me the mandate to lead strategic plan implementation for instructional technologies, broadband access, and information systems. After completing my 360-degree analysis of campus technology, I began discussing problems in their administrative operations. There was a lot of duplication of duties, which caused backlogs and delays in providing administrative services on campus. For example, telephone services, data services, and computer support were all separate departments. If you moved a staff member from one location to another, you had to deal with three departments to complete the technology transfer. Therefore, one of my first changes was merging these departments and establishing a Center for Educational Technologies (CET), later renamed Center for Technology Services (CTS).

I was allowed to establish CET in the Gordon Library, which

made perfect sense as it was a common meeting place. June Bodoni would now lead CET; she was an excellent choice as her knowledge and experience with Gordon's operations were extensive. I started working with June and the IT staff to upgrade the college's infrastructure to offer new technology services on campus. First, we established an instructional technology group to assist the professors in designing presentations (video, text, and audio). We recorded and stored class lessons so that students could access them later from on or off-campus. Next, we hired an Internet specialist to establish ISP services on campus. The reader should note that this was 2000, and the Internet was still in its infancy stage.

I was aware of the budgetary issues typically encountered when implementing such a transformational program for Gordon College. Therefore, I worked closely with selected vendors to get exceptional pricing and solicit and receive donations. I estimate that we saved approximately $2 million by my taking this approach. We acquired Xiotech storage arrays, we added wireless redundancy for the network, and we received and installed Alcatel transmission equipment. We enabled Windows and Mac equipment to communicate through the network, which was quite an undertaking. Our vendors began inviting potential clients to view our network and its capabilities. It was gratifying to see these vendors be so excited over the depth of broadband capabilities that we were offering our students and faculty. For the first time in quite a while, I was having fun and enjoying my work, but this euphoria would be short-lived once again.

As mentioned, my duties also included serving on the President's Cabinet and presidential advisory work. Jud asked me to join him for lunch one day, and we headed into Boston to a dining facility that required member status. He wanted to discuss removing certain staff members and direct reports and changing endowment investments. As I delved into the discussion, I became aware of budget constraints and his desire to build more accountability in college administration.

I did my best to help him analyze different alternatives, but he knew the final decision would be his, and I believe this was a personal struggle. A few days after our lunch, he made two employment changes, removing one person from his executive team and one person from my CET group. My perceived utopia was like a soap bubble bursting in front of me. These changes reminded me that every business has its ups and downs.

I became good friends with Jim MacDonald, Financial Director. We modeled the network costs and projected the impact of technology on college operations. Jim had excellent modeling and analysis skills. By working with him, I quickly gained an in-depth understanding of the college budget, which was important since Jud asked Elaine and me to join the executive team for an out-of-office retreat in Southern Maine. At this retreat, I felt a part of the executive team and tried to contribute to different financial and planning meetings. In addition, Elaine and I enjoyed the interactions with the staff and their spouses during extra-curricular activities.

I also formed beneficial alliances with many of the faculty members during the technology upgrades. They took an interest in the project and enjoyed our interactions. For example, on one occasion, a faculty member suggested that I apply for a public-school superintendent license in Massachusetts, as I might want to use my technology and broadband skills to help public school districts. I did take his advice and became certified as a school superintendent, business administrator, and business teacher. As an aside, I later also filed in Georgia and obtained similar credentials.

I also became a donor to the college's Partners Program, a program designed to cover the gap between accepted student tuition cost and their payment shortfall. Unfortunately, several students could not afford the tuition; however, this program made it possible for them to attend Gordon College. My participation as a Partner was gratifying. I attended several meetings where these students made presentations about how much the financial assistance had helped them pursue their educational endeavors within the freedom of faith. As you can readily appreciate, I enjoyed my college contract assignment, but the time to make a new choice was quickly approaching.

After the executive retreat, Jud asked me to join him for a lunch meeting. The meeting was high energy, and Jud was excited about all that we had accomplished together during our three-year relationship; however, I was not ready for what happened next. Jud offered me a full-time executive position to lead campus technology as Vice President. The compensation was attractive, and the benefits would have been better than any benefits previously received in my career. Wow, why did he not mention this before the retreat? I am sure I would have accepted the position; however, recognizing that this position funding was not in the annual budget, I could not accept adding the burden of this new position to the college's budget, so I respectfully declined the offer. I have pondered and questioned this spur-of-the-moment choice many times since our special lunch meeting that day, but looking back, I know I made the right choice as my next endeavor would be equally important. A few years later, Jud passed away after suffering from cancer. I attended his funeral and understood the outpouring of love given by the many admirers, friends, and family. He was an inspirational person, and I am glad that our paths crossed in life.

Tennessee Walking Horse Breeders' and Exhibitors' Association (TWHBEA)

After my experience at Gordon College, I opted to initially look at non-profit and educational opportunities for my next ERC consulting role. I prepared and sent proposals for three administrative positions for which I was certified. However, since I did not have the requisite experience to accompany my certification, my efforts were unsuccessful. However, our research into non-profits introduced a new opportunity that piqued my interest. After researching the Tennessee Walking Horse Breeders and Exhibitors Association (TWHBEA) and the industry, I approached them to become their interim CEO/Executive Director. The Executive Committee of the Board of Directors were long-time Tennessee Walking Horse enthusiasts and had enjoyed success raising, showing, and selling their horses. This committee, led by Jerrold Pedigo, shared that they sought a transformational CEO to lead change within the industry. Unfortunately, the industry's success attracted a new cadre of horse trainers who used unconventional and harmful tactics to train the horses, a process called soring. I was to work with the USDA to help reduce or eliminate these practices while elevating the breed's value.

We negotiated the terms of a contract, and I took over the Association's leadership in early 2007 (Mid-South Horse Review, 2007). Never in my wildest dreams would I have expected this opportunity to be like hitting a hornet's nest with a bat while standing there waiting for the bees to attack me. TWHBEA was started in 1935 and served as the breed registry and membership association. I quickly learned that by transformation, the committee meant a turn-around situation. The actual Board of Directors consisted of 116 members, and about one-half were in favor of industry change, leaving the other half at odds with the change. More on this in a moment.

As in previous positions, I applied my 360-degree analysis to determine the course of action needed to accomplish the wishes of the executive board members. My five-point strategy was to gain broader acceptance of our riding programs for kids, expand the interest in our instructor certifications, increase membership in the Association, increase circulation of our industry magazine, Stillpoint, and gain support for our breed's value beyond just as a show horse. Little did I know that my strategic effort would only last a year.

We used the magazine to emphasize the TWHBEA academy and Futurity and gain support for the humane treatment of horses during their training. I visited with farms and attended shows to support this strategy but quickly realized that there was growing dissatisfaction with our work by several owners and trainers. The USDA officials started attending shows and making arrests, which further fractured the industry. The detestable practice of soring was behind the formation of a competing association, the National Walking Horse Association, which led to a lawsuit by TWHBEA for copyright infringement and other infringements. Yes, I never expected these new challenges when I joined the company.

Fortunately, I was able to gain support from the National Park Service (NPS). They endorsed the Tennessee Walking Horse as the official horse of the National Park Service – yay! In preparation for the upcoming "contentious" board meeting, the Director of NPS made a video recording about the endorsement, which was complimentary of our breed and its value as a trail horse. However, due to the political games played at the annual board meeting, they did not play my video. The board meeting was the closest to a brawl that I have ever witnessed. The lack of decorum was unbelievable; however, in the end, the executive committee that hired me was not re-elected, and a new committee that did not support my previous hiring mandate was elected. You can imagine what happened next. At least I received my contract severance, which, after selling the home we purchased at a loss, enabled us to break even for the year I served as their CEO. This endeavor was just another example of why placing my trust in individuals is complicated. I know for a fact that Mr. Pedigo believed in me and our strategy, but his control and my control over the organization were short-lived, which was unfortunate. I will always value my relationship with Jerrold Pedigo; he was a true friend, and I still miss our interactions.

Destination Imagination, Inc. (DI)

In December 2008, I applied for the CEO position with Destination Imagination, Inc., located in Cherry Hill, New Jersey. My application was of interest to the Search Committee, and they reached out to schedule an interview in mid-December. The interview call went exceptionally well, and I enjoyed discussing the history of the organization and the forward-looking ideas they shared for their next CEO. The company was founded in 1983 by a professor at Rowan University. His goal was to teach creative problem-solving to students, enabling them to become productive at problem-solving. I accepted their employment offer in April 2009, intending to relocate to New Jersey and assume the CEO role on June 1, 2009. The Board of Trustees, led by Ms. Brownie Mitchell, offered me a contract that explicitly discussed the authority associated with my role and the agreement term. Although the period was not multi-year, I chose to pursue the opportunity. At first, we rented a home near the office, then after my first contract renewal, we purchased a home in Haddonfield, approximately five miles from the office.

The company's primary revenue came from team registration fees and an annual creative problem-solving competition hosted in May over Memorial Day weekend. Each year, 800 to 1,000 elementary through college student teams, approximately 5,000 students, would travel to Knoxville, TN (the host city), to show their solutions to one of the annual six challenges DI offered. The challenges were in the following categories: Technical, Scientific, Structural (later changed to engineering), Improvisational, Fine Arts, and Service Learning. In addition to being appraised on their selected challenge solution, the student teams received an "instant" challenge to demonstrate their mastery over the soft skills advocated in the program's curriculum. Dr. Fritz Schwenk was a volunteer for DI who led a team that masterfully developed the instant challenges each year. The instant challenges were fun and thought-provoking. In addition, they required flexibility and quick thinking, which are notable attributes of intelligence. I later added instant challenge awards to recognize those student teams that excelled with these challenges.

Another feature of the DI program was pin trading. This activity enabled students to learn the art of negotiation and for shy students to have an opportunity to meet and converse with other students. Dr. Nina Schwenk led the design and pin development at the DI corporate level, and each affiliate director would annually also design and develop their unique pin. Pin trading was a highlight of tournaments, and the students learned the art of bartering to obtain the sought-after pins. In addition, the international affiliate pins challenged students to engage with many students who did not speak English. I appreciated Dr. Schwenk's dedication to the pin trading program. I believe she had a sample of every pin created by the DI organization.

The DI organization was lucky to have two such dedicated volunteers administer the Instant Challenge and Pin Trading components; however, this was not unusual. As I later learned, thousands of dedicated volunteers gave time and money to ensure that children understood the creative problem-solving process. Licensed state and country affiliates administered the DI program. Each affiliate had to meet the financial and tournament requirements mandated in DI's affiliate license agreement to become licensed. In addition, affiliates were responsible for recruiting volunteers and sponsors during each tournament season. To put this in perspective, when I left the employ of DI, we had grown to seventy global affiliates with more than 30,000 volunteers. The program was a progressive tournament structure allowing students to earn the right to advance to Global Finals. Their challenge solutions needed to score in the highest level at the regional, state, or country tournaments to advance to Global Finals. The affiliate directors certified the highest-ranking teams in the tournament structure.

Each year, DI contracted with the University of Tennessee for logistics, which included arranging for dorm and hotel rooms for our student teams, their supporters, and volunteers. NxLevel Solutions, led by Pete Sanford, provided our programming and audio/visual support. Mr. Sanford was the critical ingredient in our mix of partnerships, as his work with the organization spanned more than thirty years. His knowledge of video solutions and his experience with DI made him a valued asset to the organization. In addition, the leadership of DI had many years of experience putting on the event and working with project-based contractors. DI's corporate staff consisted of several experienced executives: Ms. Maureen Donovan, who led store operations and human resources; Mr. Kevin McDonough, who was all things operations; Mr. Rusty McCarty, who led event programming; Mr. Joe O'Brien, who led finance and accounting; and Mr. Charles Bell was over information technology. The rest of the staff had specific support roles, and they masterfully accomplished their goals.

I attended the May 2009 event, and the student solutions, volunteer support, and the staff's expertise in executing the event impressed me. As an addition to the event's opening ceremony, the Search Committee requested that I make a presentation. I must admit that speaking to more than 10,000 people was unnerving for me; however, this was not the only challenge I faced during this time.

The morning we were to leave for Knoxville for the Global Finals event, I completed my usual three-mile jog. Afterward, we loaded up the car and began our trip. A couple of hours into the drive, I started feeling a pain in my stomach, but I shrugged it off as being a pulled muscle from my run; however, the pain became worse after we arrived and checked into our hotel. Elaine and I went down to supper, and the pain became so intense that I asked her to take me to the hospital. After being admitted, the diagnosis was a ruptured appendix and peritonitis, a bacterial infection. In addition, the peritonitis treatment resulted in my gaining over ten pounds from fluid retention.

Ms. Brownie Mitchell, the DI Board Chair, was so empathetic during this difficult time. She was encouraging and thoughtful. She wanted to present her new CEO to the DI community but would only do so if I felt strong enough. So, since I felt much better, I left the hospital ready to meet everyone. I was placed in a wheelchair and parked in the lobby of the Hilton Hotel. There I met with senior DI volunteers, and together we laughed at my unfortunate start with the company. However, the swelling was significant due to the weight gain from water retention, and it was not going down. A doctor on location was concerned that the swelling in my legs could be a symptom of congestive heart failure. I went back to the hospital, and I received a diuretic to help drain the excess fluids. This treatment worked, which alleviated other health concerns, and I fit into my clothes again. I believe this story will live in the archives.

As in previous endeavors, the first thing I worked on was a 360-degree analysis of the organization to determine the appropriate changes needed to align DI's strategy and resources with its market potential. This process was illuminating and stressful. I learned the company was not well funded, and their internal dynamics were in disarray. Therefore, not having the luxury of time, I immediately developed a funding prospectus to solicit corporate donations and developed a plan to try and bring all the factions (board, staff, affiliates, and volunteers) together under a single banner. We altered our mission and vision to align with creativity and imagination, which more appropriately represented our actual operations. We later changed our mission statement to "teaching the creative process from imagination to innovation." Most of our Affiliates rallied around this change. However, a few Affiliates continued with creative problem-solving as their mission.

I noted in my 360-degree analysis that goal orientation, teamwork, critical reading, research, project management, budgeting, imagination, curiosity, design principles, and presentation skills were outcomes as student teams developed their challenge solutions. However, for some unknown reason, DI was "not" highlighting these benefits in their current marketing literature. Instead, they were only presenting the principles of creative problem solving, i.e., divergent and convergent thinking. As a result, students would only focus on techniques to generate multiple solution options and then learn how to choose one or more options for their problem solution. By highlighting the added value of teaching the creative process, these previously unmentioned unique and valuable learning skills would be at the forefront of our expected outcomes for student teams.

Due to the nature of my short-term contracts, I had to operate under one- and two-year periods between renewals. Understanding the risks of my contract not being renewed required me to ensure that any strategic changes to our operations would need to have an immediate "positive" impact. It would have been nice to just focus on DI's turn-around, but due to my contract non-renewal risk, I also needed to keep my industry options for future employment open for consideration.

Fortunately, the funding prospectus brought in $75,000 from GE and an additional $15,000 from other sources. Our new strategy to re-launch the organizational mission away from being solely about creative problem solving to teaching the creative process was successful and achieved broad support among our Affiliates and school districts. The change also enabled us to differentiate ourselves in the STEAM (science, technology, engineering, art, and mathematics) educational market and align with the Partnership for 21st Century Learning's framework. In addition, I was able to add academic staff to better support our challenge writers while also adding digital marketing support to re-establish our brand to align with teaching the creative process. Mr. McCarty was excellent at business development. He established synergistic sponsorships with the National Dairy Council, AEM, and Capital Area Reach that also contributed to the funding needed to sustain and grow our organization.

At the time, DI had a few international licensed affiliates. I sought to add several more affiliates to expand our programming into schools worldwide; however, our efforts were not succeeding due to our primarily U.S.-centric perspective. Only one other person on our Board of Trustees had lived and worked abroad, so thinking with an international perspective was foreign to them. Yes, I used the word "foreign" to show my humorous side. To make our challenges more appealing outside of the United States, DI needed to offer them in international formats, allow for pricing in foreign currency, and offer the purchaser language translation. We engaged an international strategic development consultant, Ms. Renee Rainville, to develop a phased approach to achieving a global perspective. Her first great suggestion was to launch an international invitational, which would invite students from the U.S. and other countries to international locations for cultural and educational exchange. This suggestion received support, and we implemented this new strategy in 2016, with Beijing China becoming our first invitational. In 2017, our second year for the invitational, Wroclaw Poland was chosen as the location. As a result of Ms. Rainville's advice, we successfully increased our licensed international affiliates to more than thirty by the end of my tenure with DI.

There were several affiliates that I will never forget. Texas, led by Ms. Sue Shanks—one of the search committee members that hired me—was our largest affiliate. Sue's leadership was inspiring, and I enjoyed our relationship. Other affiliates that come to mind are New

Hampshire, Massachusetts, Georgia, Virginia, Ohio, California, and Poland. Honestly, Poland was one of my favorite affiliates, maybe because of our unique interactions. Ms. Margaret Jastrzebska, the Affiliate Director, continually brought exceptional students to our Global Finals. I became the advance party for the Poland Invitational—mentioned above—and pre-established working meetings with company executives in Poland who might help with funding, offer services and volunteers or provide marketing support for this initiative. Never in my wildest dreams would I have imagined the unique experience I would have in Poland.

Shortly after arriving at the airport, Ms. Malgorzata Keson, a guide, and translator greeted me. Her English was perfect, and she was intelligent and knowledgeable about American culture. In just a short time, we became like two old friends who had not seen each other in a while. I enjoyed getting to know Poland through her eyes. Malgorzata took me to all the meetings I had established before my arrival. Her business development skills became evident as we pitched different companies to support the invitational with funding or tours. For example, we could get 3M's manufacturing facility to arrange student tours through their manufacturing facilities and showroom. We met with the Project Management Institute's Poland Chapter leadership and invited them to the Invitational. Ms. Jastrzebska also joined us for several meetings to introduce me to their existing supporters and sponsors in Government and industry. When we did not have any scheduled meetings, Malgorzata took me sightseeing to memorable destinations, including the Uprising Museum. I wish I could have spent more time in the country to help our Polish Affiliate; however, it was time to prepare for the upcoming July 2017 Board meeting, so I needed to return to the office.

Many situations at DI are still memorable to me today. I remember challenging my leadership team to come up with value-add programming for our Global Finals teams. Mr. Rusty McCarty came up with the idea of adding an Innovation Expo to our offering. He and his team did a fantastic job of implementing this new program, and it was well-received by our DI community. Another memorable event was in 2011. We worked with NASA Education to bring an astronaut to Global Finals to introduce students to spaceflight and career opportunities at NASA. Mr. Leland Melvin, the Associate Administrator for NASA Education, was a former NFL wide receiver and a veteran of two spaceflights (STS-122 in 2008 and STS-120 in 2009). He was in space for more than 565 hours and traveled approximately 97-million miles. He was not only a welcome addition to our event; he became a rock star to the students. His intriguing and personal style resonated with everyone.

At the end of our Global Finals Competition, we hosted a graduation ceremony to celebrate the students who wanted to graduate at Global Finals rather than with their school classes. Mr. Melvin was the keynote speaker for this ceremony. He spoke about the Columbia tragedy and stressed how important it is to continue the crew's legacy and honor their memories through exploration, education, and inspiring the next generation of explorers.

Mr. Melvin was physically fit, which was unfortunate for me. When the students crossed the stage to receive their graduation diplomas, the guys would jump into our arms or give us a chest bump. Leland had no trouble managing this physical interaction, but one hefty college student jumped into my arms, and I almost dropped him. Later, I discovered that this catch resulted in a hernia, and I had to have an operation to repair the damage. If you have a chance to read about Mr. Melvin's visit to Global Finals, you can access it through the NASA.GOV website: (Leland Melvin and Destination Imagination).

My eight-year tenure with DI did result in several positive outcomes: we acquired, remodeled, and outfitted a new 10,000 square foot corporate headquarters and paid off the mortgage note;

we automated the Global Finals registration and housing system; we developed an online training program for new volunteers; we increased our global coverage by adding new Affiliate organizations and doubling revenues; we enhanced liquidity with a $1.3 million credit facility (the line was unused at the time of my departure); we added essential academic and marketing staff; we increased staff compensation to market rates; we doubled student participation from 75,000 to more than 150,000 students; we added an extra day to Global Finals enabling more teams to show their solutions; we added an innovation expo to Global Finals to introduce and give students hands-on experience with emerging technologies; we created the International Invitational to offer cultural exchange opportunities; and we developed new funding and academic partnerships. These partnerships were vital to validating DI's programming and commitment to student success in school and life. Some of these partnerships were: NASA's educational division, NxLevel Solutions, the University of Tennessee, Visit Knoxville, the Jeff Bezos family, Share Fair Nation (they later changed their name to Mind Spark Learning), the Buzz Aldrin Foundation, Disney, and the Project Management Institute's Educational Foundation. Lastly, I championed our foray into the Internet of Things, artificial intelligence, and robotics. Mr. Charles Bell and I developed a skunkworks group to study and research these areas. This group began developing applications, which could become a new type of program challenge and potentially enhance our Global Finals Innovation Expo; unfortunately, this effort ended with my departure from DI. Looking back, I believe that my efforts enabled DI to become more sustainable and prepared for future business challenges. Hopefully, the next chapter in DI's history will be as bright as this last chapter.

Thomson-McDuffie Middle School

After moving back to Georgia, I told Elaine that I would look for an endeavor that would allow me to return home every night. Since my Destination Imagination job required me to be away from her so much, I decided to look for open positions in educational districts near our home. The TeachGeorgia website had a posting for a teaching position at a middle school in Thomson, Georgia, approximately twenty minutes from our home. I applied and was accepted to teach Foundations of Engineering and Technology. I took the certification test for this curriculum and passed at the professional level, enabling me to be considered highly qualified for the position.

The class periods made it difficult to teach a project-based curriculum as each class was only forty-five minutes in duration. However, over time, I aligned my teaching objectives to this time constraint. Another way I was able to help bring success to my effort was to fundraise. I obtained a $1,000 grant from the electric coop that serviced the area and received a $500 donation from Pitsco, which enabled the purchase of solar and wind-energy kits.

If the kids started to get to me with their attitudes, I could always spend a moment with Ms. Anita Cummings, our principal, to regain my composure. I taught across the hall from Mr. Jay James, the business teacher. He and I had fun working together on technology issues and teaching strategies. I must say that I enjoyed my time at the middle school. The staff was committed to helping our students succeed and let them know each day that they were loved and valued. I taught at the school for the 2018-19 school year, and even though they offered me a contract for the next year, I chose to pass on the opportunity to begin writing this autobiography. However, I appreciated what the Principal wrote in my final evaluation for the school year:

Dr. Cadle has been instrumental in implementing the standards and goals of his content. Students experienced relevant situations, which made them knowledgeable of our progressive society. Hands-on projects were meaningful and relevant. His many contributions to the students and staff were immeasurable.

Lessons Learned

The opportunity to work at Gordon College was indeed a blessing. My broadband experience, coupled with my project management skills, enabled me to contribute to the future of the college. It is so rewarding to see that my efforts to establish technology as a learning asset are still a strategy for them today.

DI challenged me in many ways, but I am humbled to have had the experience. The important lesson for me in this role was when you commit to an organization, do not let internal politics distract you from your purpose, even if it means that you will ultimately have to leave the organization.

My time at TMMS enabled me to teach students critical soft skills and technology principles. I never envisioned myself as a teacher, but I am glad to have had the chance to try something new and succeed. I wish someone had taught me the creative process, problem-solving, teamwork, active listening, and discernment as a child; hopefully, you will make sure your children learn and practice these skills.

CHAPTER 9

The Blessing of My Family

Haven't you read, he [Jesus] replied, that at the beginning
the Creator made them male and female, and said, For
this reason a man will leave his father and mother and
be united to his wife, and the two will become one flesh?
So they are no longer two, but one flesh. Therefore,
what God has joined together, let no one separate.

—MATTHEW 19:4–6.

A life remembered through pictures. This recognition was my feeling as I scanned through the seventy years of photographs, videos, and mementos in preparation for this book. Other than the pictorial recap of my career ventures, I should characterize the remainder of these pictures as a view into our Christmas holidays and birthdays. These were the times when everyone had smiles and appeared to be enjoying life, but the real stories took place between these celebratory times. Smartphones have allowed us to capture photographic and video memories at any time. Another benefit of technology advancements is to enable digital storage and retrieval from all media sources. Currently, my family's pictures and videos are in several plastic bins and boxes. At some point, I will venture to scan the images and convert our reel-to-reel tapes to digital storage, but for now, all I can do is try and categorize them into some productive order.

Elaine

I met Elaine, my future wife, at Six Flags over Georgia (Atlanta area amusement park) in 1966. This chance encounter came just after I ended a long-distance relationship with a girlfriend in Washington, D.C. Elaine and her sister, Donna, were at Six Flags together with their parents. I was there with my cousin Tommy and my parents. Tommy and I noticed that these young ladies seemed to be alone, and after calming our fear of rejection, we approached them to share some rides with us. I partnered with Donna and Tommy with Elaine, but the entire time we were together at the park, anyone would have noticed that Elaine and I were a couple of goofballs. Like me, she was a non-conformist, and I loved her from the moment we began exposing our silly sides.

Elaine was intelligent and was doing exceptionally well in high school (Honor Roll/Beta Club). Elaine was attractive with long brown hair and a smile that would make you melt. She was president of the French Club and an accomplished equestrian. Her dad spoke multiple languages and had a great job with Equifax. Her mom was well-read and was always talking about topics in the news. Besides her sister, she had two brothers—Davy and Tommy. Their family had a unique relationship, and I could readily see they enjoyed their time together.

A short time after Elaine and I were married, her brother Tommy died in a car accident at the age of twenty-two. Unfortunately, the car's driver fell asleep at the wheel resulting in the vehicle swerving from the road and crashing into the highway's median, resulting in Tommy's death. I cannot imagine the devastating impact of this news on this close-knit family. Nevertheless, Tommy enjoyed his short life to the fullest extent before he died. One of my fondest memories relating to Tommy was his love for ice cream. One evening, I noticed him going upstairs, and with a closer look, I saw that he had a *large* bowl of ice cream, and the ice cream was at least two inches above the top of the bowl.

Like Elaine, her friends were also intelligent and well-rounded, and I could see the special relationship she had with them. I enjoyed becoming her boyfriend and hanging out with her family and friends. Her grandparents were also interesting people. On her mother's side, Ginny and Gramp were two special people. Gramp was the service manager at a local Cadillac dealership. He played the banjo and always had side projects underway. Ginny taught Sunday School for many years, and she was a devout Christian who could recite many Bible verses. She also used the Bible as her file cabinet for remembering birthdays and special events. On her dad's side, Mimi and Papa, who were also devout Christians, were self-educated and wise. Papa was into philosophy and audio recording. He had written several manuscripts on life, which I found interesting. He also had years of real-time recorded broadcasts on his reel-to-reel tapes, including Kennedy's presidential inauguration speech. I kept these tapes in three large bins thinking that they would be great collector's items, only to find out years later that they were worthless.

During high school and technical college, Elaine worked at the Credit Bureau of Augusta. She studied medical transcription at college, enabling her to become a medical transcriptionist with the University Hospital's radiology department. Later, when my career choice required a move from Augusta to Atlanta, she landed a position with Aetna Health Plans, a job she enjoyed for ten years. Elaine was good with numbers and common sense. She developed an Excel budget program that management valued, leading them to decide to launch the program regionally. Unfortunately, her expanded role as

Financial Coordinator for the Southeast region often required long hours, tight deadlines, and overnight travel. When I accepted a career opportunity in the Boston area, she elected to decline a company transfer, including a promotion, and instead elected to retire from Aetna. Although she expressed excitement over the opportunity for new surroundings and more time with our children, I know this was a difficult decision for her. This transition is just one example of the many sacrifices she has made for our family.

Elaine and I dated approximately four years before getting married in June 1971. We had an incredible honeymoon at Daytona Beach, Florida. Every day with her was exciting, and we were also best friends. To avoid being teased about our romantic ventures in Florida, she made sure that we left Florida with a suntan. How long is too long in the sun? We wished we had known the answer to this question because we received awful sunburns, so bad that we each had blisters and avoided touching each other due to the pain. The funny memory here is I had rented the honeymoon suite in a hotel on our way back from Florida. Even the movement of the sheets was painful, but we laughed about our "sunburns."

Before leaving this topic, I believe this would be an opportunity to insert a funny story that happened right after we rented our first house. Thinking about this rental house will always invoke a memory. We had seen some mouse droppings, so we put out a few mouse traps in the kitchen. One night just after we had gone to bed, we were awakened by dreadful screams. As I peered around the corner into the kitchen, I saw that our mousetrap had caught the tail of a sewer rat. Every time the rat tried to escape through the hole he had found in the kitchen, the trap—being a tad larger than the hole—would keep it from escaping, and this must have hurt. The rat would scream each time it tried to escape. I went back to our room to find something to hit the rat with, only to find Elaine standing up in the middle of the bed. We were both frightened, but when I took my boot and started hitting the rat as it was still running around the kitchen, I became petrified. Fortunately, its tail separated, allowing it to bolt out of the house. I immediately found ways of blocking that hole, but I must admit that the light stayed on in the kitchen after that incident.

Alicia

We were enthusiastic about starting our family; however, Elaine had trouble getting pregnant, so the doctor suggested making charts and registering her daily temperature. When you ovulate, the hormone progesterone causes your temperature to rise, and this would be the time she could conceive, so he let us know that we should be diligent during this period. Finally, a couple of years after we were married, the miracle of creating a baby happened, and we could not wait to hold this future bundle of joy.

Have you ever had those moments when you feel as if God jokes with you? Well, having this baby was one of these times. Elaine was a planner, and she prepared for this baby. She read books on raising children, books on breastfeeding, and she designed and crafted a room to become the nursery. My simple job was to choose the clothes I would wear and ensure the car was ready when the birth time arrived. I had the car tuned up, and I was ready—or at least I thought I was. Surprise! Her water broke, and the time had come to put our plans into action. However, our brains reached an overload point:

Elaine: What clothes should I wear to catch the water?

Me: Where was that perfect shirt that I was going to wear?

Elaine: How far apart are the contractions?

Both of us: Five minutes, are we going to make it to the hospital in time?

Recognizing that time was of the essence, I helped her into the car to start our short journey to the hospital, or so I thought. As soon as I gave the car gas, it would choke and quit running. When I made it to a long sloping hill, I would let the car coast to the bottom to avoid the car's engine shutting down. Our conversation again went to concern:

What if we do not make it to the hospital in time?

What if the car will not restart?

How will we contact someone for help—cell phones were only a dream at this time?

Although the drama was extreme, we made it to the hospital, and a few hours later, Alicia Gail Cadle was born on July 23, 1974, three years after we were married. Now the fun would begin—our implementing Elaine's book knowledge in contrast to our parents' experience. Elaine would try to explain different procedures she had studied in Dr. Spock's child-rearing books, only to face opposing points of view. It was stressful, but Alicia survived the competition.

As I looked at Alicia's smiling face in our holiday and birthday pictures, I remembered a time when she was not so happy. Working at Georgia Railroad Bank provided me with certain financial benefits such as reduced interest on construction loans. I used this benefit to build a beautiful contemporary home on a lake in Evans, Georgia. The house was so energy efficient that the Georgia Power and Light Company gave us an energy certification. Our primary purpose for building this house was to sell it for a substantial profit. Two years later, we decided to put the house on the market and immediately received an excellent offer. One night before the closing date, I was completing the various punch-list items. This list included a note to install a wall light in Alicia's bedroom, so I installed a nightlight next to Alicia's bed. A few days later, we explained to Alicia, who I believe was about eight years of age at the time, that we would be moving. Tears immediately came to her eyes, and she said, "Daddy, you just gave me a nightlight for my room. I do not want to move." I deeply felt the emotional trauma she was experiencing. This experience helped me become more sensitive to her feelings, and I promised her that her next room would have a nightlight.

Alicia was competitive and never ran from a challenge. She was a great big sister to her brothers, but if one of them aggravated her, she would quickly remind them who the boss was. I found several pictures of her holding or playing with her brothers, which brought back some old memories. I know her brothers love and respect her, and you can see this each time they get together.

Like I mentioned above, she was not afraid of a challenge. She became a black belt in taekwondo and a red belt in American karate, and it was fun watching my son Jeff try to spar with her. We, unfortunately, lost her black belt test video, but I still remember watching three boys with black belt rank try to attack her during the test. She balanced on one foot and had the other leg poised in a roundhouse position. The guys did not stand a chance, but they tried to get at her. I sure wish we still had that video as it was a day that she had proud parents and grandparents. Her grandparents had traveled a significant distance to watch the event. This blackbelt test was the first time they had seen her perform Karate, and they were amazed to see her break boards and defend herself so skillfully.

One of my most memorable funny events happened during her high school years. For her first car, I purchased a 1973 Corvette from a family friend. The car needed many repairs, and my dad attempted to get the car in good running order; however, even though the car was running okay, other issues kept happening. One day, she was stranded in the road because a wheel came off. Another day, the car would not start, causing the battery to run down. Buying this car was not one of the best choices I have made. Despite the issues, there also were some laughs. One that immediately comes to mind is Alicia placing her head outside the car window when she was required to pick up Jeff, her "aromatic" brother, after football practice.

In high school, Alicia was well-liked and was often involved in school projects. Her talents and social skills have always amazed me. I remember working late the night of the school's homecoming event to prepare the financials that were due the next day. Alicia was a candidate for homecoming queen along with several of her friends. I kept receiving calls from people "in the know" asking when I would arrive for the event. I quickly finished my project and left the office, arriving just in time to be rushed to the football field to stand next to Alicia. As I took my place, an announcement came over the loudspeaker. My daughter became the homecoming queen for this 3,000-student high school. Wow! As I watched her getting the school picture made with the other contestants, I stood in awe. At that moment, I realized that not only was she beautiful, tall, and talented; she was also my hero. After that night, I knew my daughter was going to achieve great things in life.

After high school, Alicia went to the Savannah College of Art and Design (SCAD). She was a talented artist, and while at SCAD, she met and later married Peter, who was also a talented artist. At this writing, Peter has a senior position with a division of AT&T. They have two handsome and accomplished boys who have achieved several sports awards in wrestling and baseball. Like me, Alicia had entrepreneurial inclinations. She founded a preschool learning center and adopted the Reggio Emilia approach to learning for her academic program. Her strategy and skill with students enabled the school to become a welcome addition within the local community. Its level of success helped her to open a second school that also thrived. She honored me by letting me help her structure both the business formation and its sale several years later. I realize that I am blessed to have such a wonderful daughter, beautiful inside and out.

Jeff

Jeffrey Charles Cadle was born on March 20, 1978. He was a healthy and happy boy. One memory of his time as a little boy was his passion for playing the Smurf video game. He would sit in front of the TV, still in his footed pajamas, and play that game for hours. Another memory is of him riding a three-wheel electric motorcycle in the house. We would constantly have to remove him from under the dining table and free him from objects he would run over.

Jeff was different from Alicia. He was more laid back, and you could readily see how much he enjoyed playing with her. She loved to carry him around and to make him laugh. Jeff also loved to tease her until she would chase after him. One vacation day in Florida, we were walking to a store after it had rained. He started kicking water on Alicia, and after she warned him to stop, he continued without fear of retaliation. Then, without any warning, she grabbed him and forced his face down in the water. Jeff was so surprised, but she demonstrated her superiority that day. We had many laughs during the years while watching them play together.

Starting in eighth grade and continuing through high school, Jeff played for a football team on both offensive and defensive lines. He took football seriously and worked out constantly. During his senior year, he was the starting center for the Foxboro Warriors in Foxboro, Massachusetts. It was amazing to watch him hike the ball and block players weighing significantly more than him. Elaine and I looked forward to his games and especially looked forward to the Thanksgiving Day games, a tradition in the area.

During his senior year, his team ended up one win away from competing for the Division 3 championship. We were anxiously waiting for this game, and it was worth the wait. The opposing team was up 7 – 0, and Jeff's team drove down the field and scored a touchdown in the last seconds of the game. The team collectively decided to go for two points rather than kick a field goal for a tie. The ball snapped, and the quarterback scrambled to find an open receiver. At the last moment, he threw the ball to a player in the end zone. With the ball about to land in the receiver's hands, an opposing player leaped and managed to tip the ball away at the last second. It was a heart-wrenching loss for Jeff and his team, but it was undoubtedly one of the most memorable games I have ever watched.

After high school, Jeff decided not to continue playing football and to focus on his degree studies. Instead, he chose to pursue a mechanical engineering degree and not continue playing football. Northeastern University had a co-op program, allowing him to obtain practical work experience in his field of study. This work experience enabled him to land a position with MKS Instruments as a junior engineer. Fast forward eighteen years, and he is now an engineering manager for the company in one of the many product development groups. I had the opportunity to listen in on one of his staff meetings while we were on vacation together. His technical knowledge, communication and project skills, and leadership skills made me proud.

On February 2, 2002, at 2:02 PM, Jeff married Andrea McCabe, who he met through our church's youth group, and they have blessed us with two intelligent and funny grandchildren, Riley and Tyler. We enjoyed going to church and spending time with Jeff and his family while we lived in Massachusetts. Jeff and I still have frequent telephone calls allowing us to keep up with each other's lives.

Jeff is talented, not only as a phenomenal dad and engineer but also as an accomplished guitarist. He has played the electric and acoustic guitars since 8th grade. Most of his practice has been for the worship team at church. Thinking back to when he was growing up, I would never have imagined the amazing young man he would become. My lesson learned here is never to underestimate a child's abilities and aspirations. His childhood experience was in an environment different than mine, yet in my mind, I only pictured the barriers I had faced and not the opportunities he might enjoy.

We were content having a boy and a girl, but sometimes life throws a curveball. I remember coming home from work one evening to find this fantastic dinner prepared. Oh no, I thought, what special occasion have I forgotten? As I was racing through my memory banks, Elaine let me know that she just wanted to make something special. Whew, now I could just enjoy the meal. After dinner, we walked outside and sat down on the deck steps. The evening was perfect, and I was enjoying the weather and the time with Elaine. As she sat down next to me, she mentioned that she had something important to tell me. Little did I know that evening's news would change our lives forever.

Jason

Jason Robert Cadle became the first of the Cadle family to be born outside of Augusta. He arrived at Shallowford Community Hospital, near Dunwoody, Georgia, on February 15, 1983, which was just what the doctor wanted. He had previously explained to Elaine that he planned a special Valentine's date with his wife on the 14th and asked Elaine not to have her baby on that day—mission accomplished. It was fun to watch Alicia and Jeff hold him and do things for him. They did all they could to play the role of big brother and sister.

We moved to Marietta, Georgia, when Jason was about three. There was a park nearby that had a lot of playground equipment. I would hoist him up on the various playground attractions, and he would giggle with excitement. I took many pictures of him playing on that playground. His long blonde hair and big smiles made excellent photographs, and we still love looking at them today. I know that

God put him into our lives for a purpose. He has always had a unique perspective on reality, and he is a natural storyteller. Jason could describe in minute detail any experience, and he could do it in such a way that pulled you into his story. Over the years, this skill has not diminished, and I can see the same trait developing in his son, Nathan.

As Jason grew up, we discovered he had spatial intelligence for both music and carpentry. Elaine had a piano in the house, and Jason took lessons on it for approximately one year. He received a keyboard for Christmas, and it was fun to listen to him play. He also developed an interest in the guitar, and we got to hear him master Van Halen songs. His musical abilities, spatial intelligence, and emotional traits enabled him to play the guitar and piano with passion. Even when he was learning to play these instruments, he never seemed to have a technical approach. Instead, he had a keen ear for the sound, allowing him to know the correct notes to play instantly.

To provide Jeff and Jason a dedicated place to practice, Elaine and I decided to add a music room and an entertainment space in the basement. Jason worked with me to build out the basement, which I believe may have been a catalyst for his later becoming interested in construction and carpentry. After completing the basement renovation, Elaine and I enjoyed listening to our boys play the keyboard and guitar in their new music room.

After he graduated high school, Jason attended technical college to seek an architectural degree. His knowledge of and experience with the building trade enabled him to easily pass the Massachusetts state general contractor's and construction supervisor test to obtain his builder's license. Earning this license was a huge accomplishment, and Elaine and I were so proud of this recognition of his experience and knowledge. After receiving his construction credentials, he started his own construction company, *Precision Carpentry and Design.*

It is difficult to recount the number of construction projects that Jason has completed over the years, but I have two projects that I will never forget. The first one happened while Elaine had been in Georgia for several months caring for her ailing parents. At the time, we lived in Attleboro, Massachusetts. I spoke to her one evening and learned that the situation was progressing in such a positive manner that she would return home in approximately a month. So, Jason and I decided to surprise her by remodeling the sitting room next to our master bedroom. Over the next month, we completed a myriad of projects: we added a master bath, we built a walk-in closet and make-up area, we restored a clawfoot tub and installed it, we pulled up the carpet and added hardwood floors, we put up walls to create a closet, and we painted the entire area. The project took the whole month to complete, working a minimum of fourteen hours a day.

Although it was a significant undertaking, we finished it just as Elaine's flight landed. Jason and I will never forget the tears running down her face when she saw what we had done. This moment was memorable and one that Jason and I will never forget. The second story that I would like to share with you was one of humor. Jason and I were working on the house that my son Jeff now owns. We would often find old newspaper articles as we removed walls and operated under the house. One day as we were adding insulation under the kitchen, we found a newspaper from 1950. An article told a story of a naked woman who was flashing cars as they passed by. The article then reported that the police were finally able to locate and apprehend the woman and that they were holding her for "observation." We laughed about that story for quite some time.

Jason now works as a pattern maker with an international slurry pump company located near Augusta. I have seen the enormous wooden patterns that he constructs, and I must say that they are impressive. He truly is the best carpenter that I know.

At this writing, Jason is the father of a seven-year-old boy, Nathan, a true blessing to us (like all of our grandchildren). Nathan was born with a severe heart condition, but the doctors did repair his heart, and hopefully, he will never have any additional problems. Only a year after his surgery, he now runs around with more energy than the Energizer Bunny. Jason married Christina, whose down-to-earth approach to life, positive attitude, and love for Jason are qualities we treasure.

Pets

I would be remiss if I did not write about our family pets. Yes, pets are family too, and although they are not children, they become embedded in family dynamics. For example, Elaine and I acquired two wonderful dogs right after we were married. They loved us so much that they would find creative ways to get out of the fenced structure that separated them from us. Unfortunately, their Houdini-type escapes became so frequent that we had to give them up—a decision I have always regretted.

For most of our kids' lives at home, we had a Pomapoo named Snuggles. He was intelligent and had a knack for knowing how to interact with each of us. One funny story was his dietary issues. Sometimes, he regurgitated his dinner and would get a towel or sock to place over his throw-up. Not knowing this, I accused Jason of doing this to avoid having to clean up the mess even though he adamantly denied doing it. Yes, I punished him for lying about this. So imagine my emotions when I observed Snuggles go into the laundry, retrieve a towel, and use it to cover up his mess. Snuggles lived a good life, but we eventually had to put him down due to kidney failure. We met Jason for his 22nd birthday dinner that evening and decided to tell him about putting Snuggles down—a regret that I will carry to my grave. He was devastated, and we were so sorry we did not give him a chance to say goodbye before we put Snuggles down.

Losing Snuggles left a significant void in our lives, and we kept our eyes open for another pet. Elaine was shopping at the mall, and she spotted an American Eskimo puppy for sale. The store wanted $700 for her, and Elaine rushed home to get me to come to see the dog; however, before we could get back to the store, someone else had purchased her. Yet fate was a God-wink away. A few months later, Elaine went to a pet adoption event, and there was the puppy. Amid our excitement, I surmised that she must have been too much trouble for her buyers. Each time we attempted to pet her, she would shy away or duck, leading me to believe she was the subject of abuse.

Nevertheless, Elaine immediately jumped at the chance to adopt her. This little dog became Elaine's best friend and support for all the time I was away for work trips. We named her Eskie, and she was an ingenious animal. As an example, she would watch TV and bark at the animals used in commercials and programming. She could hear a tune introducing a commercial that she knew had a dog in the picture and would come running and barking from wherever she was in the house. Eskie lived with us for fifteen years before dying of cancer. We miss her every day!

Lessons Learned

I am grateful and blessed to have such a talented wife and children. Looking back, each of them has made my life unique in more ways than I can recount. There are so many fond memories of our time together, but I would be remiss if I did not say that they were not all positive. I now recognize that I could have been a better husband and dad.

The only advice I can impart at this stage of my life is not to let career and finances get in the way of allowing each member of your family to know that they are deeply loved. I have since learned that the best way to interact with children is to help them find their unique voice and use positive reinforcement. For example, if you have anger issues, pursue counseling, and never discipline a child when you are angry. I now understand the importance of talking through problems and concerns. I can only imagine how much closer my family, friend, and work relationships might have been if I had learned this approach much earlier.

CHAPTER 10

Developing a Global Perspective

.... Love your neighbor as yourself. Love does no harm to a neighbor. Therefore, love is the fulfillment of the law.

—ROMANS 13:9–10

The many perspectives associated with politics are of interest to me, and even more concerning are the inflexible mindsets of some individuals and groups. Ideological fixations that lead a person or group of people to ignore common sense or be closed-minded to other views have always interested me. Why would anyone not be willing to at least listen to a person with an opposing viewpoint? Are they afraid that their perspective may be challenged and possibly make them question their assumptions? Would their worldview be threatened by having the flexibility and freedom to challenge or change their mindsets?

I realize that some viewpoints are a result of indoctrination. A student trusts a biased professor and adopts the professor's worldview. Perhaps an employee depends on their leader or coworker and adopts their point of view. Maybe a person is raised in a cultural environment that has embraced particular ideological perspectives. There have been times during my life when I have seen a simple discussion turn into an emotional event just because someone questioned another's perspective. As I am writing this manuscript, we are nearing a Presidential election. As I listen to different media reports, I find myself amazed at the misleading and biased perspectives. I wonder why anyone would want to be a politician in our current political environment. The distrust of political leaders makes it difficult to choose a candidate to support. For me, I can only support a candidate that closely aligns with my values and perspectives.

Fortunately for me, I have visited and worked in thirty-three countries, giving me the first-hand opportunity to see linguistic anthropology in action. From my experience and education, I have learned first to seek to understand others and to respect their worldviews. Honestly, you can learn so much by listening to people discuss their feelings and beliefs, assuming they are willing to have discourse.

I mention the importance of having an open mind due to my early experience of not having one. Can you believe that after more than fifty years, we still are addressing racial injustice? I grew up when segregation laws existed, which were in effect until the late-1960s (my teenage years). I looked for a website that might offer a realistic summary of segregation in the south and discovered this site: https://aapf.org/segregation. This segregated culture was so ingrained in me that I just accepted it as reality and ignored any opportunity to change my perspective. My friends were all white (Caucasian), and we avoided any association with anyone different.

I remember May 1970. I was nineteen and still living at home. A sixteen-year-old Black teenager, who should have been in the care of the Youth Detention Center, was incarcerated in an adult jail, and while detained, he died from a beating on May 9th. Two days later, on May 11, riots broke out in retaliation for the murder. Augusta buildings were being burned and looted. That night, my dad took me into our living room and posted me at the front door. He gave me his shotgun and told me to shoot anyone coming through the door. I will never forget that night. It was one of the most frightening experiences of my life.

My education and global travel have benefitted me in very impactful ways. After I earned my teaching certificate, I taught at two mostly Black middle schools. I remember the Assistant Principal at East Augusta Middle School sharing a memory about how loud horns would go off at 6 pm in North Augusta (just over the bridge from Augusta in South Carolina) to alert Black people to get off the streets immediately. I can only imagine what it must have been like to be raised Black during the Segregation period. It is not surprising that I later received reverse discrimination from Black teachers and administrators raised during this period; however, I remembered my cultural experiences and have always treated my coworkers with respect and an open mind. I think many people may have missed an opportunity to gain a different perspective. I wish my early years included interactions with more diversity of people, thinking, and culture.

Lessons Learned

As mentioned above, we are in the midst of a Presidential election and experiencing protests and riots over racial injustice while at the same time experiencing the life-changing impacts of Covid-19. This coronavirus has upended our economy and personal lives. This disease has no cultural boundaries. Maybe one of the positives of this disease, along with the protests for racial justice, is that these events might bring awareness to cultural divides and change our perspectives and worldviews toward viewing each life with love and concern.

I believe that this time in history is a wake-up call for all of us.

First, we need to stop seeing people as components of categories and start seeing them as unique individuals who deserve the right to be treated equally. Second, we may disapprove of other people's actions, beliefs, and demeanor, but we can at least respect the person's right to his or her opinion. Lastly, I have always learned to try to disagree without being disagreeable. We cannot always predict what is going to happen, but we can control how we respond.

Mark 12:28-31 informs us of the following: Of all the commandments, which is the most important? The most important one, answered Jesus, is this: "Hear, O Israel: The Lord our God, the Lord is one. Love the Lord your God with all your heart and with all your soul and with all your mind and with all your strength. The second is this: Love your neighbor as yourself. There is no commandment greater than these."

CHAPTER 11

Becoming a Life-Long Learner

When you pass through the waters, I will be with you;
and when you pass through the rivers, they will not
sweep over you. When you walk through the fire, you
will not be burned; the flames will not set you ablaze.

—ISAIAH 4:2

When I was a child, no one pushed me to read, yet I was innately curious about how things worked. In the book, *The Confident Student,* an active learner is defined as follows: "one who gets involved by taking notes, asking questions, participating in discussions, and joining clubs and organizations—someone who pays attention and knows what is going on in class and on campus" (Kanar, 2011. p. 17). At the young age of eleven, I joined the Amateur Radio Club of Augusta and later became an amateur radio operator (ham). I spent many hours learning radio theory by studying the Amateur Radio Relay League (ARRL) Handbook. Daily, I practiced sending and receiving Morse Code. My efforts were successful in enabling me to pass the exam and obtain my license (WN4AZX). After receiving my license, I would wake up early to contact hams in foreign countries when the atmospheric conditions were right. I firmly believe it was my curiosity and courage to explore things, like ham radio, that gave me the impetus to learn and experience new and different subject matter. This impetus propelled me to become a sort of polymath. This diverse interest in many subjects allowed me to relate to others and gain insight into their interests and life journeys.

As mentioned earlier, I struggled to find my footing in college, which led me to enter the Army Reserve. I remember it was during this time when I started understanding the importance of a college degree. After active duty, I returned to college and completed a double major in accounting and finance. A college or technical degree will help you in your career. Still, you will need to obtain licenses and certifications demonstrating your competency and experience in specific fields for recognition as an industry professional.

My work at International Marketing Services included financial and estate planning for the CEO/founder. I learned about the Certified Financial Planner designation and decided to pursue this certification to learn and gain experience with personal financial planning. After 1990, the process of obtaining the certificate changed; however, at the time, you were required to pass a series exam consisting of six modules with each module offered every four months, which meant the designation would take a minimum of two years to obtain. Once you completed all six parts and met the education and experience requirements, you qualified for the CFP designation.

At the same time as I began pursuing the CFP designation, I also studied for the Certified Public Accountant (CPA) exam. This exam took place over two and one-half days and consisted of business law, auditing, accounting theory, and accounting practice. In addition, I signed up for the Becker review course, which was an intensive in-person lecture. I spent hours at our dining room table studying for both the CFP and CPA exams.

As mentioned earlier, I left the employ of International Marketing

Services and joined Software Concepts. The job change took place during these exam time frames, and even though the purpose for the CFP exam was related to my former employer, I continued to study and take the progressive exam modules. My new job with Software Concepts was contingent on my obtaining the CPA designation. My hard work and ongoing study paid off as I passed the CPA exam and completed all the CFP exam modules.

My BBA degree and CPA/CFP professional credentials allowed me to take on various industry roles confidently. However, when I took the contract position with Gordon College, I realized that I would need to achieve advanced degrees to advance in future academic endeavors. Therefore, in late 2005, I chose to take a year off to complete my Master of Education degree in Leadership. This choice enabled me to continue to expand my academic opportunities, but I knew I would eventually have to obtain a doctorate to qualify for more senior leadership positions. This awareness became a driver for me when I had the unique opportunity to become the CEO of Destination Imagination, Inc., which I highlighted earlier.

I surmised a doctorate would enable me to gain essential knowledge and practical experience, which could assist me in overseeing curriculum development and instructional strategies for the Destination Imagination (DI) program. In addition, I felt an ethical duty to ensure that our challenge curriculum was written and administered in such a way as to enable students to gain the requisite skills to become both efficacious and effective in solving our challenges. A necessity for our program was to challenge students to learn the creative process and gain vital team-building skills, self-awareness and confidence, project management skills, topical experience, and entrepreneurial attributes. I had an innate drive to find new and different ways to achieve this purpose.

I realized that goal awareness and perseverance were essential factors for completing our long-term challenges. This recognition piqued my interest and ultimately became the driver behind my dissertation research. What if I could cognize a proven strategy that would motivate DI teams to stay the course and persevere through roadblocks? This strategy could become an important lesson and become actionable research that teachers could use to practice and perfect thinking techniques for goal accomplishment. This research goal became my singular focus, and I could not wait to begin the process.

Two mentors provided me the constant encouragement to persist in my studies, Dr. Amanda Rockinson-Szapkiw and Dr. Nancy Wingenbach. Dr. Wingenbach was a DI Board Trustee, and she was instrumental in helping me obtain the grit and perseverance to complete the doctoral journey. One time during my coursework, she sent me a desk set with *Dr. Cadle* inscribed on it. She never let me lose my focus, and I am grateful and blessed to have had her encouragement. Dr. Rockinson-Szapkiw was a professor at Liberty University who later became my dissertation chair. She was so skilled and intelligent, and I worked hard to gain as much knowledge as possible from her. After completing my doctorate in education, she honored me by letting me co-write a chapter in her book, "Navigating the Doctoral Journey: A Handbook of Strategies for Success." (Rockinson-Szapkiw & Spaulding, 2014).

My coursework at Liberty University was primarily online; however, several of the courses were intensive and required me to attend classes at the university for a two to three-week period. During one of these intensives, Dr. Rockinson-Szapkiw shared statistical issues about degree success: the attrition rate for online doctoral students is 10 percent to 50 percent higher than the 50 percent attrition rate attributed to non-online students. I tried to imagine why someone spent their time, effort, and money only to drop out before degree completion. I knew my personal goal was to complete my degree program within three years; however, another professor indicated that the typical time to earn an EDD (Doctor of Education) was between five and ten years. As I channeled my fear of writing, I began to experience the emotional anxiety related to completing this marathon undertaking, just like others who quit before completion. What would it take to help students stay the course?

When my coursework was over and with the comprehensive test behind me, I began to picture an outcome that would provide a strategy for other doctoral students and me while possibly offering an improvement opportunity for the DI program. A persevering attitude should be axiomatic for the completion of long-term assignments and objectives. If students are predisposed to be easily distracted, avoid longer-term tasks, causing them to lose their drive, they would never accomplish their goals. This thought resonated with me as I thought about how so many students need feedback as immediate gratification.

Then it came to me; my scientific research should seek to determine why there was such a high drop-out rate for online students seeking advanced educational degrees versus residential students. This research could lead to solutions for this phenomenon while adding value to the DI challenge development curriculum. At this point, I became energized about the impending initiative and the wide-ranging potential for the lessons learned.

I strongly remember that challenging stage in my doctoral program when finding a dissertation chair, formulating my research questions, accomplishing a research study, and writing my dissertation became the next step. The effort seemed chimerical at the time and reminded me of the Riemann Hypothesis—the math equation that no one can solve.

I have written articles for journals and association meetings, but I have always struggled to construct that "perfect" literary exposé. Before starting the dissertation process, I read self-help articles to gain insight on writing for impact. Several informative articles suggested finding your "voice" or imagining that you are talking to an audience seeking the pertinent information you offered. Other self-help opinions suggested making outlines and creating informative titles that might launch the thinking process positively. I liked Stephen Covey's suggestion of beginning with the end in mind and liked Andy Stanley's suggestion of "path" thinking. Unfortunately, these great suggestions did not make the process any easier.

As we struggle with life's challenges to the point of losing focus, some event or some person seems to come along to help us carry the ball over the goal line. These events or people seem to just appear at the right time, and I was blessed to receive a specific nudge at one of my low points. At that point in my studies, my focus on the doctoral degree started becoming less than my focus on everything else. After buying several books for my Kindle, I love to read and especially enjoy topics that expand my knowledge and understanding of technology and spiritual education trends—Amazon recommended the book *Emotional Intelligence for the Christian* (Smith, 2012). This book was fascinating, and I had trouble putting my Kindle aside to work on my doctoral studies. Smith, an accomplished author, and a preacher, also hit a wall in his graduate program and considered quitting. He posited in Chapter 15, "My pastoral heartstrings tugged at me; I wanted to get out of academia and back into people-centered ministry. I came close to quitting." He then recounted an impromptu meeting with the dean of students, who advised him to be willing to make some tradeoffs to finish the program and receive the impending benefits. Smith continued, "I'm now eternally grateful to this man for his advice and encouragement." After reading Smith's recounting of his thought transition, my motivational drive returned, which restored my passion. Reading this book was just another special God-wink that took place in my life just at the right time.

To complete my research and dissertation, I read more than a thousand scholarly peer-reviewed articles along with many books on statistics, multi-variate analysis, wisdom, neuroscience, and educational leadership. Finally, after completing my scientific studies and responding to the "many" questions from my doctoral chair, my dissertation was finished and approved. I had successfully demonstrated that the use of neuro-educational techniques (prompting the brain to stay focused on long-term objectives) was a proven strategy to combat the high dropout rates for students seeking advanced degrees in education. You can access my dissertation through digital commons (Cadle, 2013).

From my doctoral research, I learned about the Project Management Professional (PMP) designation. As I investigated the title, I began to recognize the strong correlation to the creative process, the overarching theme of the DI program. Project management consisted of ten knowledge areas: stakeholder management, procurement management, risk management, communications management, human resource management, quality management, cost management, time management, scope management, and integration management. Each of these management areas was within the DI creative process learning strategy. As a result, I introduced our program to the Project Management Educational Foundation, and after they reviewed it, they decided to become a key sponsor – yay!

I then decided that it would be necessary for some of our staff or at least me to obtain the PMP designation to provide more credibility to our alignment with project management. After I qualified to take the exam, it took me two attempts to pass the exam and obtain the PMP designation. My team and I worked closely with the Foundation to introduce students to the project management profession. We even arranged for students to take a quiz at the end of our challenge program, and if they passed it, they could obtain a project management digital badge.

Lessons Learned

I learned the importance of becoming a life-long learner. I believe that you should always be learning something new to expand your life opportunities and career.

Try to establish strategies for staying focused long enough to achieve goals. Everyone will have short-term distractions that may tend to pull you away from longer-term objectives. If you are pursuing a long-term goal, expect distractions and plan for how to mitigate them. I learned that effort, planning, and an internal commitment not to let life distractions derail my goals were the key attributes to achieving goals.

CHAPTER 12

The Trusted Adviser: A Key Ingredient for Coherence

As iron sharpens iron, so one person sharpens another.

—PROVERBS 27:17

few years back, when UtiliCom Networks was in hyper-growth mode, I purchased a new book that I thought might help me perfect my leadership skills. *The Portable Coach: 28 Surefire Strategies for Business and Personal Success* (Leonard, 1998) was full of suggestions, statements, and ideas that were new to me. I well remember an account from the book, "It's great to affect others profoundly. But if that objective is too much *out in front*, it is going to get you in trouble. Because even though everyone, deep down, wants to be profoundly affected, no one wants to be manipulated, condescended to, or patronized" (p. 84). After reading it, I began seriously thinking about my communication style and its impact on co-workers, friends, colleagues, and family. To be effective in communications, I needed to tailor my words and style to the audience.

Ever since reading Leonard's book, I have always tried to focus on helping and improving those around me with positive and constructive communications. However, if I am honest, there were emotional events in life and work that tended to derail my efforts to do the right thing. Through my many presentations and conflicts, I learned that the way you phrase your ideas and suggestions is probably even more important than the words themselves.

I successfully communicated my vision for broadband wireless and iCloud technologies with Callahan Associates International. I later shared my vision for instructional technology as an overarching strategy at Gordon College. Then I took the CEO roles at TWHBEA and Destination Imagination. In each of these organizations, I faced situations where there would be winners and losers.

At TWHBEA, the Walking Horse industry was in turmoil, with horse owners and trainers resisting my efforts to eliminate soring, the intentional infliction of pain to a horse's legs or hooves to produce an unnatural gait. Unfortunately, I failed to get these owners and trainers to accept a new vision of how the industry could benefit from eliminating soring. As a result, I ultimately had to leave the organization due to a lack of internal support for change.

At Destination Imagination (DI), the organization was still recovering from the court-ordered break-up between OM Associates (OM) and Odyssey of the Mind (Odyssey). OM became Destination Imagination, and Odyssey became a competing organization with each company offering similar problems or challenges to teach creative problem-solving. The state and country affiliates impacted by the court order made decisions to align with either DI or Odyssey. Even though this break-up took place approximately twelve years before I took over the CEO role in 2009, the internal rivalry kept both organizations from achieving their true market potential.

The unfortunate factor was that during these twelve years, the educational industry changed its focus toward developing STEM skills in students, which included robotics, computer science and coding, smart-city infrastructure, the Internet of Things, iCloud applications, and much more. However, the board of trustees was slow to embrace what I surmised as the immediate need to update and change our curriculum focus away from creative problem solving to project-based challenges. This change would allow us to maintain and expand our market position. I surmised that because DI competed with Odyssey, the market was wide open for companies like FIRST, Discovery Education, Code.org, Girls who code, PBS Kids, Future City, and others to gain traction and become competitors to DI and Odyssey. Their messages aligned with STEM education, and they began to pull school support away from DI and Odyssey successfully. I felt a strong sense of urgency to ensure that the market understood the meaningful 21st-century learning and project-based attributes of our challenges.

Over time, we successfully changed the curriculum strategy teaching the creative process from imagination to innovation. We highlighted goal orientation, teamwork, critical reading and research, project management, budgeting, creativity, curiosity, design principles, and presentation skills as key learning outcomes of the DI challenge program. Another positive departure from Odyssey's program was DI's addition of a *service-learning* challenge. Here I tried to align our challenge writing with the United Nation's seventeen sustainability development goals (SDGs). This new challenge became a welcomed part of our curriculum, and some of these challenge solutions were so emotional, they brought tears to my eyes. These curriculum changes resonated well with the educational community and allowed DI to differentiate itself in the marketplace. As a confirmation, our team counts began to grow as more school districts began offering the DI program to students.

Since we had expanded our global footprint, I added a day to our Global Finals event to enable more teams to attend. Additionally, we included interactive and experiential technology into the Innovation

Expo at the company's annual Global Finals. We brought celebrities to the event to allow students to meet and talk with industry experts. These additional improvements gave students hands-on experience and awareness of impactful innovations in art, energy, healthcare, critical infrastructure, and technology. Although most affiliate directors, parents, donors, and educators liked and supported these changes, I was having trouble getting buy-in from our board of trustees for the changes and the "sense of urgency" I recognized. I think the board did not simply accept my suggested operational changes, and this annoyed me. I am sure there were several other times when my annoyance impacted my communication tone. I think this tone could be why the board's management committee asked me to work with a consultant to improve my communication skills. At first, this request frustrated me, but what happened next has been a blessing that I will cherish forever.

One of our board trustees, Mr. Eric Wolff, was an organizational consultant focusing on executive coaching. Eric was an extremely knowledgeable and experienced individual. He studied and lived in many different cultures, coached many executives, advised leaders at the top levels, and his perspective on organizational dynamics was insightful and engaging. Due to his proven principles, he became my communications consultant. From his Linkedin page, his bio reads as follows:

> My work is strongly focused on creating leaders capable of Cultural Change. Cultural Change cannot be gained through force or coercion. We cannot control the thoughts and beliefs of others, so Cultural Change requires something more profound. It requires leaders who are adept at gaining cooperation and skilled in the art of diplomacy, salesmanship, patience, endurance, and encouragement. It requires

leaders with the emotional intelligence of empathy and compassion. It requires a leader who knows how to see multiple dimensions of the organizations, people, and dynamics around them.

During my time working for DI, I watched Mr. Wolff successfully navigate and resolve trustee conflicts. His help in garnering support for changing DI's organizational mission enabled us to move away from the previous creative problem-solving mission to teaching the creative process. He had a sixth sense for addressing conflict with positive emotions and constructive communications. I admired and respected him as a board trustee and began to look forward to the eight sessions the board had authorized for us.

Each progressive session with him pushed me to challenge myself in new ways. After completing the 8-weeks of sessions, I felt more self-aware, self-confident, and culturally attuned, thereby improving my communication ability. In addition, I learned how to use active listening principles and to use questions to bring about positive discussions. In other words, I learned how to engage others with the end in mind so that any breakdown in communications would not derail the end goal. He was a masterful communicator, and he quickly became a trusted mentor and friend.

Later, after Eric left the board of trustees and became an employee of DI, we co-rented a house near the office that served as our home away from home. We were both commuting to DI's corporate office from out-of-state locations. Each night together, we would have deep discussions about a myriad of interesting topics. We would discuss world religions and explore differences and similarities. Sometimes, we would discuss DI and potential strategic changes. However, every discussion made me increase my appreciation for our relationship. Eric became my best friend. He has inspired me in so many ways, and I will always treasure his friendship, mentorship, and support.

Lessons Learned

I have always attempted to solve my personal or professional problems through research. However, after I met Eric Wolff, I realized how many people in my life could have provided me with guidance and unbiased advice if I were open to receiving it. Unfortunately, I think I am like a lot of us and do not want to ask for help for fear of judgment or for showing vulnerability. After my Eric experiences, I now find that I am more open to sharing with others, and I look forward to discourse. When resolving a conflict, I have also learned not to have a biased or one-sided opinion. As Stephen Covey said, "Seek first to understand and then to be understood."

The wisdom I take away from this chapter story is that like the verse at the beginning of this chapter suggests, one person can sharpen another person. So, try to find people who can provide mentoring or consulting advice to you. The person may be a religious leader, a trusted colleague, a family member, or a financial adviser. I honestly believe you will discover how good it feels to share your life burdens and receive constructive, positive, and helpful feedback. First, however, you may need to wrestle with vulnerability as I did.

CHAPTER 13

Life Lessons Learned from Volunteering

Command them to do good, to be rich in good deeds, and to be generous and willing to share. In this way they will lay up treasure for themselves as a firm foundation for the coming age, so that they may take hold of the life that is truly life.

—1 TIMOTHY:18–19

I have volunteered many times during my life and career. My first volunteer role was working at the *Masters Golf Tournament* as a Gate Guard and later as the Radioman for the tournament's movie sound crew. But, probably my most challenging volunteer role came when I worked for Georgia Railroad Bank. The bank liked its employees to be a visible part of the community. So, I had the unique opportunity to serve as the volunteer Director of Operations for the Emergency Preparedness Agency (formerly referred to as the Civil Defense).

The Civil Defense required me to study for and pass an operations exam and shadow the Agency's Executive Director. This experience came in handy when on February 6, 1980, Augusta had a significant ice and snow event. The ice made the roads impossible for regular traffic, and there were multiple accidents. As a result, I came into the Defense office after a call from the Executive Director to help with getting hospital and healthcare workers to and from their job locations. Never in my wildest dreams would I have imagined the challenge of doing this.

My first thought was how to mobilize all-terrain vehicles and volunteers to help with this task. After evaluating several opportunities, I decided to reach out to ham radio operators and owners of all-terrain vehicles to help us with transporting emergency workers. I situated ham radio operators in each four-wheel drive vehicle and at the hospitals enabling us to communicate directly over the two-meter band with the vehicle driver and hospital administrator. This way, the drivers would not have to return to the civil defense office for their next assignment. I chose to lead the radio dispatch and received instructions from the administrators about whom we should transport. For the next fifty-two hours, I worked to fulfill the needs of the hospital administrators with only a few short breaks. Our efforts enabled the hospital's janitorial and administrative staff, nurses, and doctors to get to their work locations. We only had a handful of people not reached by our team of radiomen and vehicle drivers.

After my Civil Defense position, I have held the following volunteer positions: a member of the Leadership Society for PMI Educational Foundation, Board Director for Springlakes Subdivision, Board Director for Mind Spark Learning, Board Director for Woodgate Subdivision, Ham Radio Club Volunteer, Advisory Member of the Augusta Business Advisory Council, and as a Board Director for the Partnership for 21st Century Skills. In addition, I am currently serving as the technology assistant at Wesley United Church in Evans, Georgia, where I provide networking support, serve as a camera operator, and operate ProPresenter—the church's slide and video presenter software.

Lessons Learned

I was reminded of the importance of volunteer roles when I worked at Destination Imagination (DI). This non-profit would not exist if it were not for the dedication and passion of more than 30,000 volunteers worldwide. Whenever I thought about the sacrifice of time and money this army of people made for DI, I was inspired and energized to keep the DI program relevant as a valued educational resource for schools.

I have learned the importance of offering my skills, knowledge, and experience in volunteer positions. These positions are a way of helping others just for the love of helping people. I believe volunteering keeps us grounded. Aren't we showing love for our neighbor when we sacrifice our time, effort, and money to help others achieve their goals? I think so.

CHAPTER 14

The Coherence of Wisdom: Final Thoughts

The Lord Almighty has sworn, 'Surely, as I have planned,
so it will be, and as I have purposed, so it will happen...

—Isaiah 14:24

Yes, my life has been unique, and my path paved with events I could never have imagined. Even though my childhood was not perfect, my emotional intelligence was late to develop, and my earlier trust issues prevented me from forming deep personal friendships. Nevertheless, I believe my life story has been worth writing. I am blessed to have so many memorable experiences, and I recognize their impact on my life journey.

I think some people accept their fate in life as if their path were deterministic; however, I believe most of us find a meaningful life path, even if it is by accident. The biggest takeaway from my life journey is that choices have consequences, and a critical evaluation of lessons learned from these consequences can lead to wisdom. As I am sure you have noticed, each decision made involved risk and the opportunity for failure. Writing this book has given me the unique opportunity to examine my life and gain insight into the many blessings bestowed on my family and me. I am incredibly grateful for these blessings. Listed below are a few of my most meaningful memories.

When I was a teenager:

My ham radio experience enabled me to take the role of communications coordinator for the sound man at the 1968 Masters Golf Tournament. After the tournament was over, the support personnel could play the course and use a caddy. I played the first nine holes. How many people wish they could say that they have played at the Masters? I got that chance.

While in the employ of Solid State Systems, Inc.:

My chance to buy Solid State Systems from Alcatel led me to meet Dr. Bill Gordon (a former billion-dollar fund manager). He became a colleague, friend, and valued ally in several of my career positions.

I am grateful for having had the opportunity to work with Atlanta Mayor Andrew Young and Mr. Billy Payne to provide telecom switching services to the Atlanta Organizing Committee after Atlanta was selected to host the 1996 Summer Olympic Games.

While in the employ of IBCS/A. O. Rustel:

In Russia, I worked with the former Deputy Telecommunications Minister Gyorgi Kolmogorov. I helped the founders of A. O. Rustel and IBCS, Jim Hickman and Arnie Freedman, launch satellite communications as the second carrier for Russia. The experience taught me about digital technology and broadband communications and their potential for revolutionizing networking and communications.

While in the employ of Conway Data, Inc.:

I worked with McKinley Conway, founder of Conway Data, and Ms. Laura Lyne (his daughter) to launch the World Development Corporation, which became an adviser on billion-dollar super projects to Bechtel, Flour Daniel, and other infrastructure contractors. In addition, I had the opportunity to plan and implement a well-attended infrastructure conference in Singapore.

While in the employ of Gordon College:

I worked with Dr. Jud Carlberg, President of Gordon College, and June Bodoni to implement strategic initiatives at the college. The opportunity allowed me to meet Christian scholars who provided me with unique insight into Christianity and the Bible. In addition, June became a special friend and mentor.

While in the employ of UtiliCom Networks, LLC.

I had the opportunity to work with Rich LuKaj, founder of Bank Street Holdings and former investment banker with Bear Stearns, and with Mark Rein, Chief Information Officer at the U. S. International Development Finance Corporation. They helped me learn strategies that were critical to the success of UtiliCom Networks (UCN). Their help and advice enabled me to take this company from start-up to

$25 million in profitable revenue and arrange a financing deal with Blackstone Capital for a $100 million investment.

While in the employ of Destination Imagination (DI):

I was able to form valued relationships with Eric Wolff, Sue Oclassen, Max Kringen, and Nancy Wingenbach, who became trusted advisors to me in my role as CEO of DI.

Ms. Lee Knight was a tenant in my apartment building in New Jersey. Her focus on health, her technical experience, and her MBA knowledge made the stories we shared both illuminating and inspiring. In addition, she provided me with valuable technical research, which helped with fundraising and many high-level presentations.

While on a business trip to Qatar, I had the opportunity to share an evening meal in the palace of multi-billionaire Sheikh Faisal Bin Qasim Al Thani, Chairman of the Board of Al Faisal Without Borders Foundation. Even though he was extremely wealthy, he surprised me by being down-to-earth and fun-loving. Sheikh Faisal was an excellent host, and I will never forget the special evening he hosted for my colleagues and me, showing us his antique car, rug, and cultural museums. Sheikh Faisal had spent a fortune bringing artifacts from other cultures to Qatar so that Qataris would have the opportunity to experience the world. I am glad that my life journey included this experience.

I developed a mutually beneficial relationship with NASA. Through this relationship, I had the opportunity to meet and work with three astronauts—Buzz Aldrin, Frederick Gregory, and Leland Melvin. I also worked with Dr. Roosevelt Johnson, Associate Administrator for Education, and Ms. Tammy Rowland, Manager of NASA Academic Affairs. Due to these relationships, we introduced students to NASA technologies at Destination Imagination's Innovation Expo. In addition, I had the chance to visit Marshall and Houston Space Centers to talk with the engineers involved in deep space flight. I also developed a "go-to-Mars" cartoon with Buzz Aldrin. We played the cartoon at Global Finals as part of an opening ceremony skit.

I had the opportunity to meet John Travolta. He had flown his jet to Kennedy Space Center for a fundraising event that I was attending. John and I hit it off immediately, and I enjoyed getting to know him. At the 2015 Global Finals, we hosted Paula Abdul as our guest celebrity. I discovered that she is a down-to-earth individual who is extremely smart, talented, and skilled at teaching leadership to students. The students loved her, and she was available to them for questions and comments.

My mother-in-law loved the band *Mercy Me* and asked for us to play the song *Imagine* at her funeral. So imagine my excitement when I had the chance to meet and talk with Bart Millard, who wrote and performed this song. His children were participants in the DI program.

While attending Liberty University:

I learned a sustained and undistracted effort, persistence, and grit can enable students to achieve long-term goals. I learned from Dr. Amanda Rockinson-Szapkiw, Dr. David Holder, and Dr. Jillian Wendt. Each of these people guided and supported me through my doctoral program. David and Jillian later worked as special volunteers for DI at Global Finals.

As a further blessing to my life journey:

I married my childhood sweetheart, and she and I had three children—Alicia, Jeff, and Jason—who have further blessed us with grandchildren. In addition, I had loving parents, grandparents, and an awesome brother. My Uncle Jim and Aunt Rhetta taught me so much about life, and their children Lynn, Suzanne, and Wesley have been special to me during my life.

My Coherence

Evaluating my life lessons and personal relationships, like those shared with you in this book, has enabled me to "value" and appreciate my past. Praxeology is the study of human action and behavior. From the analysis of my actions and behavior, I have learned that no matter how much you try to control your career or life situations, some disruptive event may derail your efforts. Therefore, maybe consider my approach and seek to mitigate the downside of your choices. These disruptive events also include fear. I have learned to use fear as a warning sign but not to interact with fear as an unmanageable emotion. If you manage fear, it can have positive physical and mental effects, but it can have paralyzing effects if you let it consume you. Finally, I have learned that only God is in control, so seek His will in all that you do.

I have lived through the Vietnam War, the end of segregation, the President John F. Kennedy assassination, the Martin Luther King "I have a dream" speech, the gas shortage in 1973, the O. J. Simpson chase and trial, the first moon landing, the Space Shuttle Challenger explosion, Desert Storm, the terrorist attack on the United States September 11, 2001, the financial crisis in 2008, the Boston

Marathon bombing, several shootings of congressional leaders, and now Covid-19. All these events have changed our social norms and challenged us to act and think in new ways. Who would have ever thought it would be normal to put on a mask, enter a bank, and ask for money?

I have learned that there is no perfect life on earth. Every human must chart his or her path, and I thank God for the many blessings He has provided to my family and me. Yes, I made regrettable mistakes, and I take full responsibility and accountability for them; however, I have gained wisdom from evaluating these mistakes and successes. Taken together as a unified whole, I have gained a practical perspective on life and my interaction with it. It is this coherence leading to the wisdom that I wanted to share with you in this manuscript.

I believe that the quest for practical wisdom will positively impact your family, career, spiritual, or social life. Recognize that conflict and disappointment in life are part of life. Seek to learn from all life's lessons. I am grateful and blessed to learn from my social interactions. In addition, I have gained cultural knowledge and experience from a career that gave me the chance to visit and work in thirty-three countries.

I trust that you have enjoyed my musings and reflections portrayed in this manuscript. I pray for God's blessings on you as you make choices and take chances on your journey through life. Finally, I would personally like to thank you for reading and reflecting on *The Coherence of Wisdom*. Please visit my book website at www. thecoherenceofwisdom.com. I would love to hear from you.

Blessed are those who find wisdom, those who gain understanding, for she is more profitable than silver and yields better returns than gold. She is more precious than rubies; nothing you desire can compare with her. Long life is in her right hand; in her left hand are riches and honor. Her ways are pleasant ways, and all her paths are peace. She is a tree of life to those who take hold of her; those who hold her fast will be blessed.

—PROVERBS 3:13–18

REFERENCES

Annie E. Casey Foundation. (April, 2011). Double jeopardy: How third-grade reading skills and poverty influence high school graduation. Retrieved from https://files.eric.ed.gov/fulltext/ED518818.pdf

Belemont, K. (2017). A. J. Gordon: An epic journey of faith and pioneering vision. Bloomington, IN: WestBow Press.

Beutel, M. E., Tibubos, A. N., Klein, E. M., Schmutzer, G., Reiner, I., Kocalevent, R. D., & Brähler, E. (2017). Childhood adversities and distress - The role of resilience in a representative sample. PLOS ONE, 12(3), e0173826. Retrieved from https://doi.org/10.1371/journal.pone. 0173826

Blackstone. (2000, February 2). Utilicom Networks Secures $100 Million Commitment from Blackstone. Retrieved from https://www.blackstone.com/the-firm/press-releases/article/utilicom-networks-secure-$100-million-commitment-from-blackstone

Business Insider. (April 13, 2018). The unlikely way Jeff Bezos became one of the first investors in Google, which probably made him a billionaire outside of Amazon. Retrieved from https://www.businessinsider.com/how-jeff-bezos-became-first-investors-in-google-2018-4

Cadle, C. R., 2013. *Effects of using a neuroeducational intervention to enhance perseverance for online EDD And EDS students.* Retrieved from https://digitalcommons.liberty.edu/cgi/viewcontent. cgi?article=1721&context=doctoral

Denverpost. (2000, June 8). Callahan, Compaq launch 'Net data firm. Denver Post. Retrieved from https://extras.denverpost.com/ business/biz0608j.htm

Doorn, K., Kamsteeg, C., & Silberschatz, G. (2019). Cognitive mediators of the relationship between adverse childhood experiences and adult psychopathology: A systematic review. Development and Psychopathology, 1-13. doi:10.1017/S0954579419001317 Retrieved from https://pubmed.ncbi.nlm.nih.gov/31631833/

Evansville Courier & Press. (2006, August 15). WOW acquires Sigecom. Evansville Courier & Press. Retrieved from http:// archive.courierpress.com/business/wow-acquires-sigecom-ep-449778722-324502521.html/

Glasser Institute for Choice Theory. (n.d.). What is Choice Theory? Retrieved from https://wglasser.com/ what-is-choice-theory/

Heim, C., & Nemeroff, C. B. (2001). The Role of Childhood Trauma in the Neurobiology of Mood and Anxiety Disorders: Preclinical and Clinical Studies. Science Direct. Retrieved from https://www. sciencedirect.com/ science/article/abs/pii/S000632230101157X

Internet News. (2000, March 2). Liberty Surf Buys X-Stream for $68 Million. Internet News. Retrieved from http://www.internetnews. com/bus-news/article.php/314361/Liberty+Surf+Buys+X-Stream+for+68+Million.htm

Kanar, C. C. (2011). *The confident student* (7th ed.). Boston, MA: Wadsworth.

Leonard, T. (1998). *The portable coach: 28 surefire strategies for business and personal success.* New York, NY: Scribner.

Martin, S. (1996, November 5). US entrepreneur killed in Moscow. The Irish Times. Retrieved from https://www.irishtimes.com/business/us-entrepreneur-killed-in-moscow-1.102800

Mid-South Horse Review. (2007, March 12). TWHBEA Announces New Executive Director and CEO. Midsouth Horse Review. Retrieved from https://www.midsouthhorsereview.com/news.php?id=3297

NASA.Gov (2011, June 9). NASA and the Destination Imagination Global Finals. Retrieved from https://www.nasa.gov/audience/foreducators/nasa-destination-imagination-finals.html

Rockinson-Szapkiw, A., & Spaulding, L. (2014). Navigating the doctoral journey: A handbook of strategies for success. London, UK: Rowman & Littlefield.

Russert, T. (2007). Wisdom of our fathers: Lessons and letters from daughters and sons. New York, NY: Random House Trade Paperbacks.

Shankland, S., & Ryan, J. (2020, March 29). Elon Musk shows Neuralink brain implant working in a pig. CNET. Retrieved from https://www.cnet.com/news/elon-musk-shows-neuralink-brain-implant-working-in-a-pig/

Smith, M. B., (2012). Emotional intelligence for the christian: how it radically affects your happiness, health, success, and effectiveness for christ. How to Achieve It Where It Counts Most. Damascus, MD: SilverCrest Books.

Sternberg, R. J., & Jordan, J. (Eds.). (2005). A handbook of wisdom: Psychological perspectives. Cambridge, UK: Cambridge University Press.

Wright, R. T., Strimel, G. J., & Grubbs, M. E. (2019), Foundations of engineering & technology (7th Ed.). Tinley Park, IL: The Goodheart-Wilcox Company, Inc.

Yates Electrospace Corporation. (n.d.). Home page. Retrieved from http.//www.yateselectrospace.com

Printed in the United States
by Baker & Taylor Publisher Services